STAGE RIGHT

A SELECTION OF SHORT PLAYS, SKETCHES AND MONOLOGUES FOR LADIES

– by Carol Reeve –

STAGE RIGHT
Copyright © Carol Reeve 2008

ISBN 978-184426-530-5

First Published 2008 by
UPFRONT PUBLISHING LTD
Peterborough, England.

Printed on FSC approved paper by
www.printondemand-worldwide.com

ONE ACT PLAYS

SKETCHES

MONOLOGUES

ONE ACT PLAYS

Dedicated to the ladies of Llan Ffestiniog WI whose
interpretation of *Snow White and the Wicked Queen*
enhances the cover of this book

Carol Reeve

PETTY SESSIONS

– by Carol Reeve –

CHARACTERS:

> The Clerk of the Court
> The Usher (Miss Tompkins)
> Mrs. Bagot, JP – Chairman of the Bench and upper-class dog lover
> Mrs. Jones JP – Down-to-earth
> Miss Meade, JP – Elderly, sweet-natured and deaf
> Police Inspector – Precise
> Hilda Grubb – Cockney shoplifter
> Augustine Hargreaves – Irish gypsy
> WPC Smith – Young and flighty
> Miss Pugh – Spinster
> Mrs Slagg – Her spiteful neighbour
> Agnes Crisp – Solicitor
> Mary Watson – Solicitor
> Penelope Peabody – Nervous and Welsh
> Flora Faggott – Cheerful and Scottish
> Mabel Plunkett – Scared and rather dim

SCENE: A Magistrates Court. Magistrate's bench with three chairs on platform centre back, Clerk's desk below centre, dock set at an angle down left, witness box at similar angle down right, benches for lawyers in front of each.

When the play starts, the stage is empty. Then the Usher enters DR, arranges papers on the Clerk's desk, then on the Magistrate's. Enter Clerk DR.

CLERK	Good morning, Miss Tompkins.
USHER	Good morning, Ma'am All ready for the fray?

CLERK (wryly)   I hope it wont be a fray. I don't know why, but we always seem to have twice as many cases when I've got a headache. AND it's pouring with rain.

USHER   Dear, dear. Shall I get you some aspirin, Ma'am?

CLERK   No, don't worry, Miss Tompkins - it'll wear off. My young son was given a trumpet for his birthday and he spent the entire weekend blasting our eardrums…

USHER   Not a very sensible present, was it Ma'am? Who gave it to him?

CLERK   I'm afraid I did! My husband hasn't spoken to me since. That's some compensation, I suppose! You don't happen to know anyone who'd like to buy a nice trumpet, do you? Going very cheap?

USHER   I'll bear it in mind, Ma'am.

(Some lawyers and members of the public have drifted in.)

CLERK   Who's sitting on the Bench today, Miss Tompkins? Quiet little Miss Meade, I hope?

USHER   Yes, Ma'am, and Mrs. Jones…

CLERK   Ah! "Up the workers and down with men!"   She'll frighten the rain away. But who is   Chairman today?

USHER   *(with deep meaning)* Mrs. Bagot, Ma'am… *(pause, while the Clerk sags)* Shall I get that aspirin now, Ma'am?

CLERK	Please, Miss Tompkins. My headache has suddenly taken a turn for the worse.

(Usher begins to leave, then sees three ladies arriving through the auditorium)

USHER	They're here Ma'am. *(loudly)* ALL RISE!

(Everyone stands. The ladies are chatting as they walk through the auditorium on to the stage)

MRS JONES	… six sheets and as many pillowcases - not a hope of them getting dry outside today, so there they are, cluttering up my kitchen.
MRS BAGOT	You should send them to the laundry - I always do. And they seem more wholesome when they are crisp and starchy. Don't you agree, Miss Meade?
MISS MEADE	I beg your pardon. I didn't quite… ?
MRS BAGOT	*(Loudly)* CRISP AND STARCHY!
MISS MEADE	I've never heard of them, I'm afraid. Are they a new firm of solicitors?
MRS JONES	It's no good, Mrs Bagot, she must have left her hearing-aid at home again.

(They arrive on stage, bow to the court, and take their seats, Mrs Bagot in the middle. Much shuffling to get comfortable, sorting papers, opening handbags etc. Finally Mrs Bagot nods to the Clerk. She turns and says)

CLERK	First case, please.
USHER	Call Hilda Grubb!

(An anxious person of doubtful means appears in the dock, and the Inspector goes into the witness box opposite)

CLERK	Would you state the facts of the case, Inspector.

INSPECTOR	Yes, Ma'am. *(opening note book and reading)*. On Friday the twenty-third of March, the accused was observed in the lingerie department of Messrs. Mendal Kilne. She was seen to conceal something beneath her coat, and on leaving the store was apprehended by the store detective and brought to the manager's office, where the accused was found to be wearing three dresses and two coats, all with price tickets attached, and with eight pairs of tights in one coat pocket and a pair of ladies under garments in the other.
MRS GRUBB	It's a lie!
CLERK	Mrs. Grubb, you are charged that on Friday 23rd of March you did take various garments, the property of Messrs Mendal Kilne, with intent to deprive the rightful owners of their possession. How do you plead, guilty or not guilty?
MRS GRUBB	How do I know when I can't understand a word what you're saying?
MRS BAGOT	Mrs Grubb - did you or did you not steal those clothes?
MRS GRUBB	*(angrily)* No, I flaming well didn't.
CLERK	The accused pleads not guilty, your Worships.
MRS BAGOT	What nonsense! The poor woman doesn't understand the implications. Listen to me, Mrs Grubb - were you intending to pay for those garments?
MRS GRUBB	What garments?

MRS BAGOT	*(patiently)* The three dresses, two coats, the tights and the underwear which you took from the lingerie department.
MRS GRUBB	No, I never. Don't you believe ER, lady (pointing to Inspector) You know what coppers are - bent, the lot of them. Specially lady coppers. My old man says I've been framed, and he knows all about the law.
MRS JONES	From which side, I wonder?
MRS BAGOT	Inside, no doubt! *(Miss Meade is trying to attract her attention)* What is it, Miss Meade?
MISS MEADE	I may not have understood the case clearly, but are we certain the lady was not wearing her own clothes at the time?
MRS BAGOT	Of course she was - underneath!
MISS MEADE	Underneath what?
MRS BAGOT	Three dresses and two coats with price tickets on!
MISS MEADE	Well, I often leave the price tickets on my clothes - so fiddly to remove, you know.
MRS JONES	But you wouldn't wear three dresses and two coats?
MISS MEADE	I might, if it was a very cold day.
CLERK	There were also the eight pairs of stockings and the undergarments concealed in the coat pockets, Your Worship.
MRS GRUBB	Knickers!

MISS MEADE	*(deeply shocked)* Oh! I heard THAT! Mrs Bagot, we cannot allow the Bench to be abused.
MRS BAGOT	Certainly not. Mrs. Grubb, if you do not withdraw your remark, I shall have to remand you for contempt of court.
MRS GRUBB	But I only said "knickers", didn't I? That's what they put in my coat pocket - a pair of cami-knickers. 'Orrible shade of green too. Wouldn't be seen dead in 'em.
MRS BAGOT	I suggest you plead guilty just the same, Mrs Grubb, then we can settle the whole thing here and now.
MRS GRUBB	Never! I was framed!
MRS BAGOT	Then if you persist in maintaining your innocence, I suggest you ask to be tried at the Crown Court - perhaps a jury will be more sympathetic to your case.
MRS GRUBB	Does that mean I shall be in all the papers, and on the tele? Right o then, I've decided to go for the Crown Court. *(everyone sighs with relief)*

MRS BAGOT. Very well. You may stand down. Case dismissed.

(Mrs Grubb and the Inspector leave the court.)

CLERK	Next case please.
USHER	CALL Augustine Hargreaves!
MRS.BAGOT	Augustine Hargreaves? That sounds better. We could do with a bit of class in the Court... Good gracious! What's that?.

(An old bedraggled gypsy woman appears in the dock, and a WPC enters the witness box)

CLERK	Augustine Hargreaves, Your Worship. WPC Smith will give the facts of the case.
WPC	Well, your Worships, it must have been about 12.30 this morning, well, last night actually - and I was patrolling the High Street with WPC Jenny Clark – actually we weren't exactly patrolling just then, 'cos we were looking at that huge poster of Richard Gere in the record shop and comparing him with John Barrowman - you know, the one with the gorgeous eyes - well, all of a sudden this old gypsy woman bumps into us and falls into the road. We picked her up, and she breathed whisky all over us – nasty! Anyhow, between us we managed to tow her along to the nick and the sarge booked her for being drunk and disorderly.
MISS MEADE	Poor old dear - I expect she had nowhere else to go.
MRS JONES	Nonsense. A hard day's work and a hot bath are what she needs. All layabouts should be put to work in the mines, if you ask me!
MRS BAGOT\	Well, we didn't, Mrs Jones, and please direct your remarks to the Bench, not to the Court.
CLERK	Augustine Hargreaves, you are charged with being drunk and disorderly – how do you plead, guilty or not guilty?
AUGUST H	Guilty, me Lord.

CLERK	Not "my Lord", Hargreaves - "Your Worships"
AUG. H	Guilty, Your Worships.
MRS. BAGOT	Very well. My colleagues and I had better confer.
USHER	Court rise!

(Everyone stands, and the JP's come down and walk up and down the auditorium. All sit down)

MRS BAGOT	What do you think, Winifred? A hefty fine, or a good long stretch?
MRS JONES	Well as I see it, her sort would actually enjoy the comforts of prison, so I suggest a fine of £25 or so, then she will have to get a job to pay it off.
MRS BAGOT.	Excellent! What do you think, Miss Meade?
MISS MEADE	Well, I don't think a poor old woman like that would be able to get a job -she's obviously fallen on hard times and needs care and attention. Perhaps a few days in the prison hospital?
MRS BAGOT.	Alright, we'll ask her a few more questions first. *(They go back to the stage, Usher calls ALL STAND)*. Mrs. Hargreaves - do you have a home to go back to?
AUG HAR.	I have indeed, your Worship. Where the wild creatures graze among the soft heather, and the great old trees stretch their mantled arms down to the tumbling streams… that is my home.
MISS MEADE	Oh, how enchanting! Such poetry!

MRS BAGOT	Have you ever done an honest day's work, Mrs. Hargreaves?
AUG H.	Surely to God, your lovely Worship, have I not been a humble musician these thirty years? Until that sorrowful day when winter froze the puddles into glass and wrapped its icy fingers round my feeble body… what else could I do, but sell my faithful instrument to keep myself alive with a good coat, warm food and boots? No more will generous pennies clink into my cap upon the pavement outside the grand theatres while rich music pours from my heart into the busy air…
MRS JONES	*(knowledgeably)* Ah - she was a busker!
CLERK	May I ask Mrs Hargreaves what sort of instrument she played?
AUG H	T'was the voice of the Angel Gabriel, Sir - the noble trumpet.
CLERK	Ah-ha! I do believe I might be able to assist your Worships in your decision. By sheer coincidence, a friend of mine *(The Usher clears his throat)* wishes to dispose of a trumpet, quite free of charge. Perhaps if Mrs. Hargreaves would care to take possession of it, it would enable her to make a fresh start in life?
MRS BAGOT	What an excellent idea! Mrs. Hargreaves, we shall bind you over to keep the peace for twelve months, and send you from this Court suitably chastened, I hope, yet with the generous means of earning your own living. And we shall not expect to see you in here again.

AUG H. Your Worships - kind ladies - my old heart is overwhelmed with the gladness of your charity and trust. And to show my gratitude, from henceforth I shall come and play outside this Court whenever you three virtuous ladies are in attendance. My music shall give strength to your resolution! *(She bows, and the Clerk goes to her).*

CLERK *(stage whisper)* If you would care to wait in the hall until the morning session is over, Mrs Hargreaves, I will have the trumpet brought to you.

AUG H You are most kindly and just, my lord, I will be awaiting in the entrance lobby. *(She goes)*

MISS MEADE What a delightful person!

MRS. BAGOT Humph! Next case please.

USHER Call Miss Pugh!

(A prim lady enters carrying a small dog)

MRS JONES Good gracious! Do we allow dogs in court?

CLERK Perhaps we could make a special allowance in this case, your Worships, the dog being the cause of the complaint?

MRS BAGOT I see. Yes, we will allow the dear little doggie to stay, Miss Pugh. Such a nice little chap - pedigree?

MISS PUGH Oh yes, your Worship, little Pooksie has blue blood. She is a Hertfordshire Hottentot.

MRS BAGOT Is she really? How nice!

CLERK	If I might call Mrs. Slagg who is the plaintiff in this case?
MRS BAGOT	Certainly! Certainly!
USHER	Call Mrs. Jennifer Slagg! *(lady enters the witness box)*
CLERK	Mrs. Slagg, would you tell the Court in your own words the nature of the complaint against Miss Pugh?
MRS SLAGG	Well, last Saturday I spent the whole afternoon planting lettuces in my vegetable patch at the bottom of my garden. With food prices going up and up its only right that we should grow as much as we can to help the national economy, don't you agree?
MRS JONES	How right you are! Its high time every householder dug up his tennis court and filled in his fish pond to grow food for the starving masses. Highly commendable, Mrs. Slagg.
MRS SLAGG.	Thank you. But the moment I went into the house to make a well-earned pot of tea, THAT WOMAN released her nasty little dog and sent it through the hedge to destroy every single lettuce leaf.
MISS PUGH	Oh, how could you, Mrs Slagg? Poor little Pooksie just happened to stray into your garden, dazzled no doubt by the bright orange shirt your husband was wearing as he snored in that deck chair...
MRS SLAGG	Are you insinuating that my husband is a lazy good-for-nothing?

MISS PUGH   Not at all, Mrs Slagg. However if YOU say he is, who am I to disagree?

MRS SLAGG   How dare you, Miss Pugh! And what may I ask were you doing that Saturday afternoon? No, I'll tell you - peeping and prying and stirring up trouble!

MISS PUGH   I do NOT peep and pry! I was giving Pooksie a little run in the back garden… and one would have to be blind not to see that lazy orange heap spreadeagled while you crouched over those withered lettuces like a toad…

MRS SLAGG   A toad? A toad! I… I have never been so insulted in my life! You should be locked up for using such disgusting language! And that revolting dog of yours ought to be painfully destroyed!

CLERK   Ladies, ladies! Order - please!

MRS BAGOT   Yes, this is unseemly behaviour and not to be tolerated. Besides the poor dog is shaking with fright. There, there, Pooksie, its all over now. And did Pooksie dig up those nasty lettuces then?

CLERK   Your Worship, the defendant in this case is Miss Pugh, not the dog…

MRS BAGOT   I am well aware of that…

MISS MEADE   I remember once reading about a pet tortoise that used to greet visitors by withdrawing into its shell and rolling down the garden path until it bumped into their ankles. Remarkably intelligent, tortoises.

MRS BAGOT	*(after a pause)* What on earth has that got to do with this case?
MISS MEADE	Well, I think it was the lettuces that reminded me. Tortoises eat lettuces, you know.
MRS BAGOT	Well, DOGS DON'T! So why, Mrs. Slagg, do you suppose that Pooksie should make such a vicious attack upon your lettuces, unless she was provoked by some traumatic experience, as Miss Pugh has suggested?
MRS SLAGG	Nothing of the sort. That dog is forever digging up things in my garden - daffodils in the spring, wallflowers in the summer - and then it comes in and scatters the autumn leaves as soon as I've swept them into tidy heaps.
MISS PUGH	Like I said - Pooksie is affected by bright colours, particularly shades of yellow, orange and brown. She can't help herself, poor little precious.
MRS BAGOT	May I ask if she digs up the daffodils in YOUR garden too?
MISS PUGH	Oh no! She's far too intelligent to do that!
MRS. SLAGG	No- she just heads for my garden and destroys that!

MRS BAGOT	Oh dear. It is clear to me that Pooksie is a bad girl. Do you agree? *(The other JPs nod)* Well, Mrs Slagg, we find that your complaint is justified, but we suggest that you erect wire-netting round the border of your garden. And Miss Pugh, you MUST keep Pooksie under proper control. You will be fined a nominal sum of ten pounds to pay for Mrs. Slagg's lettuces. And why not take Pooksie to your local optician and buy her a little pair of sunglasses, so that she wont be dazzled by bright colours any more? I think that should solve the problem.
MISS PUGH	Oh thank you, your Worship - you have been so kind
MRS BAGOT	*(smiling)* I think we dog-lovers have a special understanding, don't you?
MRS JONES	What rubbish!

(Mrs Pugh, Pooksie and Mrs Slagg leave the Court)

MRS BAGOT	Next case, please.
MRS JONES	I wonder if its stopped raining yet?
MISS MEADE	I hope we don't have any more animals in the dock. Its so bad for my hay fever.
USHER	Silence in Court! Call Mrs Peabody!

(The Inspector enters witness box, a lady is in the dock, and barristers and solicitors on the benches).

CLERK	Inspector, would you give the court the facts of this case.

INSPECTOR	On Wednesday the 21ˢᵗ March I was called to the scene of an accident in the High Street, where I found a red mini-car embedded in the window of Maison Clare, the hairdressing salon. The owner of the car, who had recently been driving it, was ascertained to be a Mrs Penelope Peabody. In the centre of the road lay a somewhat damaged bicycle and seated beneath a lamppost was the owner of the bicycle, a Miss Flora Faggott. Witnesses agreed that Mrs Peabody had knocked Miss Faggott off her bicycle before entering Maison Clare in her motor car by way of the public footway and a plate-glass window. She has therefore been charged with dangerous driving.
MISS MEADE	Was anybody hurt, Inspector?
INSP.	No, your Worship. No injuries were sustained, and an alcohol test on the accused proved negative.
MISS MEADE	I'm so glad.
CLERK	Miss Peabody, you have heard the charges - how do you plead, guilty or not guilty.

(Solicitor rises and speaks to the Magistrates)

WATSON	(Solicitor) Mary Watson, Your Worships, I represent Mrs. Peabody, and my client wishes to plead not guilty. I have informed her of the procedure of this and she wishes to take the Oath.
MRS BAGOT.	Very well. *(Clerk takes the book to Mrs. P who reads)*

Mrs. PEABODY	"The evidence I shall give shall be the truth, the whole truth and nothing but the truth."
MRS JONES	*(aside)* Such a pity we don't add "So help me God" like the Americans do - gives it so much more impact, I always think.
2nd SOLICITOR	*(rising)* My name is Agnes Crisp, and I represent the prosecution in this case, your Worships.
MISS MEADE	Ah- your partner must be Starchy! Welcome to the Court!
WATSON	If I might begin? Mrs Peabody, on the afternoon in question, you were driving towards the High Street on your way to the hairdressing salon. Would you tell us what happened next?
MRS PEABODY	*(very nervous)* Well, yes, I got to the traffic lights and they turned orange under the red, and while I was trying to remember if that meant stop or go coming next, this driver hooted at me from behind. Well, I got rather confused and put the car into third gear so it didn't move off very easily... then I started to go up the High Street when this woman on a bicycle that I was passing stuck her arm out and immediately began to cross in front of me. Well, I swerved and tried to accelerate past, but found myself in the window of Maison Clare - glass everywhere and at least five minutes early for my appointment.
MRS BAGOT	Very nasty for you. Have you been driving long, Mrs Peabody?

MRS P	About five years, on and off… mostly off.
MRS BAGOT	How interesting. Do you wish to cross-examine, Miss. Crisp?
CRISP	*(rising)* Thank you. Mrs Peabody, do you not feel, in the light of events, that it might have been wiser to have used your brakes and hooted your horn when the cyclist began to ride in your path?
WATSON	*(rising)* Does this question bear any relevance to the case?
CRISP	I merely wish to show that Mrs. Peabody's driving was not of the highest quality. If she had reacted differently the accident might not have occurred.
WATSON	And I wish to prove that despite those reactions, Mrs Peabody was not the perpetrator of the accident, whereas the lady on the bicycle was.
MISS MEADE	Was what?
MRS BAGOT	Hush!
MISS MEADE	I'm sorry, but I just wondered what the lady on the bicycle was.
MRS BAGOT	Perhaps we should hear her evidence next. Is that in order?
CLERK	Yes, your Worship. Call Miss Flora Faggott!

(Inspector leaves the box and Flora Faggott enters.)

MRS BAGOT	Miss Faggott, I understand that you were involved in this unfortunate accident. Would you tell us what happened?

FLORA F	Och aye. Weel, it was a beeeoootiful day - not like today, so damp and dismal.
MRS JONES	Is it still raining?
FLORA F	Aye, cats and dogs! Weel, I decided to goo to the library to change ma wee library book, and to see if they'd got in the special one I'd ordered called "Silent Spooks of Scotland". We Scots are gifted with the second sight, and I always know what's going to happen before it does! Then I saw the Library across the road so I put out ma hand and started to cross. When wham! That woman knocks me right off ma bike in the middle of the road.
WATSON	Miss Faggott, did you turn to see if there was any traffic behind you before beginning to cross?
FLORA F	Of course not! I would have fallen off! Besides, I have the second sight- I'd have known if there was any danger.
WATSON	But with due respect, Miss Faggott, the danger WAS imminent. For were you not immediately knocked off your bike by a motorist beginning to overtake you? Was the second-sight perhaps a bit clouded?
FLORA F.	Don't be facetious, young man. My second sight is in perfect working order. You are thinking of crystal balls - they get cloudy.
MISS MEADE	*(trying to be helpful)* MISS Faggott, perhaps your second sight switches itself off now and again, like a small… light-house? Or would you say it occasionally needs a new battery?

FLORA F.	Ah yes - that's much nearer the truth. Every now and again if I'm feeling a bit low, it needs a little replenishing.
WATSON	In other words, you and your second sight get run down… ? *(general laughter)* What form does this replenishing take, may I ask? Would it be some sort of liquid refreshment?
FLORA F	Och, you're not so stupid as you look! Aye, I take a wee dram to lift up my spirits…
MISS MEADE	*(shocked)* You don't mean… WHISKY, Miss Faggott?!
FLORA F	*(shocked too)* Whisky? What a terrible accusation! Demon drink has never passed my lips! No- I take a wee dram of goat's milk with a spoonful of marmite to revitalise my cycling muscles.
MISS JONES	Ugh! What a ghastly concoction – goat's milk and marmite!
MRS BAGOT	Well, I am convinced that there is a case to answer, and that it should go forward to be heard in the Crown Court. Are we agreed? *(JPs nod)* Very well. You may all stand down.

(Solicitors and clients exeunt.)

MISS MEADE	Are there any more cases to be heard this morning? My feet have gone quite numb.
MRS BAGOT	Then you'd better jump and down for a bit. *(Miss Meade does so)*
CLERK	We have one more case your Worships, that of Mabel Plunkett.

USHER   Call Mabel Plunkett!

(a very scared woman enters the dock, WPC in box)

MISS MEADE Why, its that lady constable again - the one who admires John What's- his- name . Hello, dear!

CLERK   You may state the facts, WPC Smith.

WPC SMITH Oh ta. Well, it was last Thursday, March 22nd, to be exact, when the Sarge asked me to go and investigate a report of a disturbance in a laundrette - well, there wasn't anyone else on duty so I had to go, didn't I? - when I got there I found a whole crowd of people shouting that a mad woman had locked herself in one of the washing machines, so the manager had had to turn off the electricity which meant that everyone else's washing had been ruined. Anyhow I squeezed through, and after ten minutes or so we got the woman out, so I took her down to the nick.

MRS BAGOT Was she violent?

WPC   Well no, not really. Bit on the quiet side - sort of broody.

MISS MEADE Chickens go broody…

WPC   Actually, we haven't got a word out of her yet, and we don't really know why she shut herself in the washing machine in the first place.

MRS BAGOT. I'll get her to talk. Now Mrs. Plunkett, stop being stupid and explain yourself this instant!

(Mrs. P shrinks in fear)

MRS JONES	You were a bit fierce, Mrs. Bagot. Let me try. *(patronising)* Now then dear, no-ones going to hurt you. Just tell us the truth and we wont punish you too severely. *(Mrs P shrinks still further)*
MISS MEADE	May I? Mabel… *(Mrs P looks up)* That is your name, isn't it? *(nod)* Oh good. You and I have a lot in common, you know - people get so cross with us! So let's pretend there's no-one here but you and me. Now, did you shut yourself in the washing machine? *(Mrs P mouths something)* Would you speak a little louder, Mabel , I'm rather hard of hearing.
MRS P	No. *(Consternation in Court)*
MRS BAGOT	Then how did you get in there? *(Mrs P looks to Miss Meade for help)*
MISS MEADE	Now don't get upset, Mabel. Just tell me.
MRS P	I fell in…
WPC	Well did you ever!
MISS MEADE	Take no notice, Mabel. How did you fall in?
MRS P	Leaning over. Foot slipped. Fell in.
MRS BAGOT.	Oh dear. Oh dear. Were you doing your washing then?
MRS P	*(shaking her head)* Looking for something.
MRS BAGOT	And what were you looking for?
MRS P	*(beginning to cry)* Baby's sock.
MISS MEADE	Poor Mabel! Did you find it? *(Mrs P shakes her head)*

MRS BAGOT	So you fell in - you're not very big after all, but it was a remarkably stupid thing to do. Then the door shut so you couldn't get out - Is that right? *(Mrs P nods, still tearful)* Where was the manager all this time?
MRS P	*(gulping)* In the dryer…
MRS JONES	What on earth was he doing in there?
MRS P	Looking for baby's sock…
MISS MEADE	Poor Mabel - what a terrible experience.
CLERK	Should we proceed with this case, your Worships? It seems to me that the police have no reasonable charge to lay against Mrs. Plunkett.
MRS BAGOT	I quite agree.
MISS MEADE	Just a minute - don't you think, just this once, we might have a whip round to enable Mabel to buy her baby a new pair of socks?
MRS JONES	I'm sure it's quite illegal…
MRS BAGOT	… but quite acceptable in the circumstances. Mr Usher, would you take a hat round the Court, please? *(Usher finds a hat, takes it round Court, then JPS)*
MRS BAGOT	Would you count it please, Usher?
USHER	Six pounds and thirty five pence, your Worships.

MRS BAGOT	Excellent! Give it to Mrs Plunkett. There, that should keep your baby in socks for the next ten years! I think we can honestly say that Justice has been seen to be done. Good morning, Mrs Plunkett. *(Mrs P exits delightedly, also WPC)*
CLERK	That concludes the cases for this morning, your Worships. Will you take recess?
USHER	All stand! *(JPs rise and begin to leave the stage, bowing to standing lawyers, Clerk etc. They chat as they come down through audience)*
MRS JONES	We had a motley crowd to deal with this morning, didn't we? Will you join me in the Red Lion for a draught of cider and a pork pie?
MRS BAGOT	No thank you, Winifred. I'm meeting Sir Henry at Macdonalds. How about you, Miss Meade?
MISS MEADE	Oh that's very kind of you, Mrs Bagot, but I don't like to be gooseberry. No, I shall enjoy my sardine sandwiches in the Park as usual. Why, there's that dear little Mrs Hargreaves waiting in the lobby with her trumpet. Perhaps she would care to join me?
MRS BAGOT	See you at 3.00 then. Goodbye!

(They have gone, leaving the Clerk and the Usher alone on stage).

CLERK	What a morning! After those cases, this afternoon's will seem positively dull, whatever they are.

USHER   I've just realised, Ma'am, why this is called the Petty Sessions - not one of those cases was what you might call "important".

CLERK   Don't you think so? They did perhaps lack historic proportions, and certainly won't make the headlines in tomorrow's papers, if they are mentioned at all. But to the people involved… well, I doubt if their insignificant little worlds will ever be quite the same again. On the whole, I think we saw the quality of mercy dropping like the gentle rain etcetera et cetera… which reminds me, I wonder if its still raining outside? By the way, my headache's completely gone, Miss Tompkins!

USHER   Oh I am glad, Ma'am. Shall we follow the ladies?

(They leave the auditorium, leaving the court empty. Lights down.)

CAST AROUND
– by Carol Reeve –

A one-act play for 6 women

CHARACTERS in order of appearance:
>Mrs Emily Fitzwilliam – Undertaker's wife, meek and mild
>Mrs. Flora Girton – Postmistress, busy-body, always teasing
>Miss Madge King – Receptionist for the doctor she idolizes
>Mrs. Downing – Vicar's wife, chairman of Ladies Group
>Mrs. Christie – Young-executive wife, always plays the lead
>Miss Zena Clare – Retired actress, invited to produce next play

Scene : A room in a parish hall. Six chairs and a small table. Tuneless singing is heard off-stage (e.g. "When I am laid in earth", Orfeo). Mrs Fitzwilliam enters with a tray of cups , saucers, milk, sugar, tin of biscuits, which she arranges on the table and removes the biscuit tin lid. As she begins to arrange the chairs into a wide circle, Mrs Girton enters.

MRS GIRTON | Good evening, Emily – first again, I see. I hope you've brought some of my favourite assorted biscuits… oh, yes! I'll just have one of those Bonbons before that Christie woman sees them.

MRS FITZ. | Oh Flora! You shouldn't! There's only two this week, and the others will notice.

MRS GIRTON   No they won't – not if I eat the other one as well. There! My goodness, it is bitter outside . According to that Fish man, we're going to have snow next week. That should be good for your Harold's business, anyway.

(*She takes off her coat and hangs it up*)

MRS G (cont)   Which reminds me – old Mrs. Newnham hasn't been into the post office to collect her pension again this week – perhaps you had better send your Harold round with his tape-measure just in case.

MRS FITZ.   (*shocked*) Oh Flora, you are awful! You shouldn't joke about things like that. I don't know why people make fun of Harold and his profession – what would you all do without undertakers to arrange your final journey when you have to leave your loved ones behind?

MRS GIRTON   Take a taxi? No, I'm sorry. Emily, I'm only teasing. You're too sensitive, that's your trouble. And so… so humble as well. You remind me of Uriah Heap and his mother – ever so 'umble they were.

MRS FITZ.   I don't think I ever knew them… were they the Heaps of Little Sodbury who made a fortune out of sludge and organic rhubarb?

MRS GIRTON   (*Laughing heartily*) Oh Emily! You say the most ridiculous things. No Uriah Heap – you know! Dickens? Oliver Twist?

MRS. FITZ.	(*Biting her lip*) No Flora, I don't. I never had the benefit of a private education like you.
MRS GIRTON	Now, now, Emily – don't sulk! The trouble is you have no sense of humour! I don't think you would recognise a joke even if it was neatly laid out in a coffin!.

(*Enter Miss. King*)

MISS KING .	Coughing? Who's coughing? Oh poor Emily – is it your chest again? You ought to rub on that Ammonia Chloride Linctus – Dr. John absolutely swears by it.
MRS GIRTON	I'm not surprised – it smells absolutely disgusting!
MISS KING	Have you tried it then, Flora? Yes, it does remind one rather of blocked drains in hot weather. But Doctor John always says "the more revolting it is, the more good it does". Take Mrs. Robinson and her knees. For example – one bottle of Panelixir and she was running up and down stairs like a mountain goat! Mind you, it didn't do her knees much good, but it worked wonders for her vertigo.
MRS. FITZ.	There's nothing wrong with my chest, Madge. You mis-heard. But Flora was just saying that old Mrs. Newnham hasn't been seen around lately – is she poorly, do you know?

MISS KING   What, old Mrs. Newnham from the cottages? Dear oh dear – she hasn't been to Surgery, not that I know of. I hope she hasn't had a recurrence of her little Trouble. She always gets it when the wind is in the East. Mind you, I don't think Tom Jones helps much.

MRS GIRTON   Who?

MRS FITZ.   I beg your pardon?

MISS KING   Tom Jones – you know! (*she wriggles her hips*) Mrs Newnham goes to the Over Sixties Disco every Friday – they only have two records that the Vicar bought at the Brownies Jumble Sale. "The Best of Tom Jones", and "Stomping With The Folk Weavers" – but that's a little warped now. You should see the old dears doing the Salsa to "Delilah"! Mind you, they're all in the Surgery next morning with their slipped discs. Dr. John makes me laugh – "Here they come!" he says, "Those gyrating geriatrics!"

(Mrs Girton laughs. After a pause -)

MRS FITZ.   I don't think that's at all funny.

MISS KING   Oh. He doesn't mean it in a nasty way, Emily. But of course he does like his round of golf on a Saturday, so he tries to get through his "bodies" as he calls them, as quickly as possible. He gives all of them that Ammonia Chloride Linctus I was telling you about – marvellous for aches and pains, broken legs, dizzy spells…

MRS GIRTON   Oh, you do go on so, Madge. As long as everybody's ill you're on top of the world! You two and your "bodies"… *(she laughs suddenly).* If Dr. John can't patch 'em , Harold will dispatch 'em! *(She thinks this is hilarious, but neither of the other two join in – they are offended. Mrs. Downing enters.)*

MRS DOWNING   Hello ladies – I'm sorry I'm late - the Vicar got caught up by his bell ringers… I've brought the plays – are we all here and ready to start?

MRS GIRTON   Apologies from Mrs. Selwyn – she came into the post office yesterday to send off her nephew's parcel of clean underwear, and told me that she might not come tonight as she was expecting one of her hot flushes.

MISS KING   Ah! She wants to put her feet into a bucket of cold water. Always works. Dr John is a great believer in shock treatment.

MIRS GIRTON   It's a wonder he has any patients left to shock!

MRS DOWNING   Now, come come ladies, we're not going to start quarrelling again, surely. We have a lot of work to do tonight. Mrs. Christy is just parking her Range Rover on the bowling green, then we can start before Miss Zena Clare arrives. Oh, I forget to tell you – Miss Clare has agreed to produce our next play – isn't that wonderful?!

MRS FITZ.   I'm awfully sorry, Mrs Downing, but who is Miss Clare?

MRS GIRTON   You mean "who WAS Miss Clare". Where
              were you thirty years ago? I can remember
              when she was in Sodbury Rep, before she
              went to Clacton to understudy St. Joan.
              Not a bad actress really. Considering her
              shape.

MRS DOWNING   She still is, Mrs. Girton. She has a regular
              walk-on part in "Home and Away". She
              lives in the village now, and I felt we
              needed someone who didn't belong to the
              Group who would really mould us into
              something... *(very meaningful)*. She is
              Equity, you know.

(Enter Mrs Christy)

MRS CHRISTY   Oh, here you all are. Some idiot has been
              watering the bowling green, and I've got
              mud all over my stilettos... Look what I
              found knocking on the broom cupboard
              door!

*(Miss Clare enters – a real theatrical entrance. There is a quick
burst of applause)*

MISS CLARE   How NICE of you to invite me! I do
              apologise for keeping you waiting. If this
              kind lady had not rescued me, I might
              have been discoursing with a dust-pan all
              night!

MRS DOWNING   I'm SO glad you could come. Shall we
              have a cup of tea while we get to know
              each other? Emily – kettle! *(Mrs Fitz exits)*
              Let me introduce you – this is Mrs.
              Girton, our postmistress. *(They shake hands,
              Mrs. Girton muttering about Sodbury rep)* And
              this is Miss King, who has an incredible
              gift for curing our ills... *(they shake hands)*

MISS CLARE   How very interesting – I must speak to you later about my budgie's cornutations.

(Miss King looks pleased – then perplexed)

MRS DOWNING   And finally this is Mrs. Christy – our leading lady!

MRS CHRISTY   Hallo again. Yes. I have played Juliet at the High School, Portia and Titania with the little Sodbury Thespians, and recently Elvira with the Institute Players.

MISS CLARE   How very nice for you! *(Gently)* But did you play with sincerity?

(Mrs Fitzwilliam enters with the pot of tea. Goes to table and begins to pour.)

MRS DOWNING   Oh, I nearly forgot! This is Mrs. Fitzwilliam, wife of our local funeral director. She is the mainstay of our little Group, making tea, prompting, painting scenery, running up curtains…

MISS CLARE   My my! Such energy! I wonder if we can find you a part to play on stage this time. *(Mrs Fitz. is overcome as she hands out cups)*

MRS DOWNING.   Well now. We have selected one or two short plays, but we haven't decided which one to perform – perhaps you would like to choose, Miss Clare?

MISS CLARE   No, no! I'd much rather hear you all read first. Just a few lines from each one if you like, to give me some idea of your … er… er…

MRS GIRTON   *(sarcastically)* Limitations?

MISS CLARE   Well, rather say potentialities – though we shall see, no doubt.

MRS DOWNING Very well. If you're ready, Mrs Christy and Madge – how about the beginning of "Diamonds are for Evelyn"?

(Mrs Christie and Miss King take scripts and come downstage

MRS CHRISTIE *(shades of Edith Evans)* "Mary – Mary – come here, girl. Lord Flutter is awaiting me in his hansom below, and my diamond necklace seems to have mislaid itself from my velvet-lined rosewood coffer. Find it at once, girl"

MISS KING   "Yes yes Madam, at once. No, it is not in your velvet-lined rosewood coffer, Madam, and yet I swear I put it there myself not half an hour since. You put it on the dressing table."

MRS CHRISTIE *(crossly)* No, no – "not half an hour since YOU put it on the dressing table… "

MISS KING   No dear – it says here that YOU put it on the dressing table…

MRS DOWNING Yes, yes – very good ladies. Very good. *(Miss Clare is hiding a smile)* What do you think, Miss Clare? It's quite a thrilling drama, isn't it? In the end the necklace is found, all dissolved in a glass of champagne!

MISS CLARE   Really? How ingenious! I'm afraid I nearly mistook it for a farce. Might I suggest that we try it again with – yes, Mrs. Fitzwilliam as the Countess, and Mrs. Christie as Mary? *(consternation!)*

MRS FITZ.   Oh, but I couldn't! I mean, I never do any
                   acting anyway, not that I wouldn't mind,
                   but…

MRS CHRISTIE   (*interrupting*) The very idea! I couldn't
                   possibly take the MAID'S part… whatever
                   would my husband's managing director
                   think? Clive is up for promotion, and Mr.
                   Madingley always comes to see my plays.
                   No, no – quite out of the question.

MISS CLARE   Yes, it is a very difficult role. But I should
                   like you to read it, just this once. Please?

MRS CHRISTIE   (*grudgingly*) Oh, very well. Come along,
                   Emily!

*(They stand stage front, and this time the play is revealed as a
thriller)*

MRS FITZ.   (*very quietly*) "Mary – Mary, come here girl.
                   Lord Flutter is awaiting me in his hansom,
                   below, and my diamond necklace seems to
                   have mislaid itself from my velvet-lined
                   rosewood coffer. Find it at once, girl."

MRS CHRISTIE   (*cruel and sarcastic*) YES. Yes, Madam, at
                   once. No, it is not in your velvet-lined
                   rosewood coffer, Madam – and yet I swear
                   I put it there myself not half an hour since
                   YOU put in on the dressing table."

MRS FITZ.   "I particularly wished to wear it this
                   evening. Please make a thorough search
                   while I am out. I shall have to wear my
                   pearls after all."

MRS CHRISTIE   "Yes Madam, of course. While you are out
                   I shall search this room from top to
                   bottom. No drawer will be spared."

(Miss Clare claps her hands)

MISS CLARE   There – now wasn't that good? SO different. You wouldn't believe it was the same play. I am beginning to enjoy myself! Shall we try something else?

MRS DOWNING   Well, we had wondered about this one – it's a farce.

MISS CLARE   Oh dear!

MRS DOWNING   Or perhaps this little drama, entitled "Stormy Petrol".

MISS CLARE   I don't know that one – is it about sea birds?

MRS GIRTON   No – its about a ship that runs out of petrol during a storm.

MISS CLARE   My goodness! Do you think we could manage to build a ship in time for the Festival? And wouldn't it be rather a cramped set?

MRS GIRTON   No, no! The action takes place in a fisherman's cottage by the seashore. Everyone's waiting for news – all the wives are knitting and remembering how their fathers never came home, with fog horns blaring, eerie music, and a submerged cathedral tolling under the sea… lovely!

MRS DOWNING   Mrs Girton's choice, "Stormy Petrol". There is a big dramatic scene for her as Grandma Macgonagle. In fact there are eleven big dramatic roles altogether.

MISS CLARE   Do you have eleven members in the Group?

MRS DOWNING	Well, no – but the characters keep coming in and going off so we could double up…
MISS CLARE	I see. I wonder if we should try the farce – first?
MISS KING	What a good idea! It's about a hospital waiting room, and there's a lovely part that I SHOULD like to try – if you don't mind!
MRS CHRISTIE	She wants to be the receptionist, would you believe? There is one rather meaty character that I'd like to do – the patient waiting for the hysterectomy. Should be great fun – plenty of pathos and pity. (*she takes script and comes forward to read, very dramatically*) "It's too late now… to say sorry, I didn't mean all those terrible things I said. Because I love you… tomorrow perhaps? Or will it be too late…? Oh… George!" (*she collapses on her knees, weeping loudly. everyone applauds, except Miss Clare*)
MISS CLARE	Can you get up, dear? Oh good. Very moving. But I don't think that part should be played for laughs. Now, I wonder what Mrs. Downing would make of it?

(Consternation again – some scoff, others complain)

MRS DOWNING	I don't wish to be awkward. Miss Clare – but really I'm too old for that part; it needs a younger person, someone with poise – sensitivity… on dear, someone who isn't big and bossy like me!
MRS FITZ	Oh, Mrs Downing, you're not at all bossy! Why not try… ?

MRS DOWNING Oh dear – very well. I'll have a go. (*She takes script, and paused momentarily before beginning, quietly, simply and from the heart*) "Too late now … to say sorry. I didn't mean all those terrible things I said. Because I love you… Tomorrow perhaps? Or will it be too late?...oh, George"

(*When she finishes, everyone is very still*)

MISS KING That was lovely, Mrs Downing, lovely! (*Aside to Miss Clare*) She had that operation last year, you see – wonderful recovery.

MRS FITZ Would anyone like a biscuit?

MRS CHRISTIE Please. What, no bourbons again? Really, Emily, just because you're a tea lady and general dog's body that doesn't entitle you to pinch the best ones before the rest of us arrive!

MRS GIRTON As a mater of fact, "Elvira", it was me – I had them, and I shall do the same again next week. You'll have to make do with the digestives.

MRS CHRISTIE Oh you… you parsimonious old postmistress! I shall post my parcels in Plimpton from now on!

MRS GIRTON Three cheers! And I won't let you have your family allowance – not until you apologise to Emily!

MRS DOWNING Ladies! Ladies! Please! I have a much better idea – in future, Mrs Christie can be in sole charge of making the tea and buying the biscuits – and perhaps she could bake some of those delightful fairy cakes that go so well at the Bring and Buy?

MRS CHRISTIE	Oh, alright then. I'm sorry, Emily. (*She smiles*)
MRS FITZ	That's quite alright, Mrs Christie – may I call you Elvira?
MISS KING	You mustn't mind us girls, Miss Clare- we have a little squabble now and again, but it's not serious. Actually, its symptomatic of environmental apathy, according to my Doctor John. You know – the change of life. It creeps upon us once we're past thirty, and bothers us with cramps, and flushes, and migraines, and tennis elbows, and goodness knows what else! I was telling them before you came in – nearly everything can be remedied either with a cold shower or a bottle of Ammonia Chloride Linctus.
MISS CLARE	Oh yes – I seem to have heard of that. Now, who was telling me? Oh of course – poor Mrs Newnham who lives next door but one. She bought a bottle for her "troubles", whatever that was. Somebody recommended it – and just look at her now!

(There is a deathly hush. Everyone is looking at Miss Clare.)

MISS KING	Yes?...Yes?...Oh – do go on!
MISS CLARE	Well, she's in hospital, isn't she?
MRS GIRTON	I told you so! She'd never miss coming in for her pension on a Tuesday unless something terrible had happened.
MISS KING	Perhaps she damaged something at the disco?

MISS CLARE	Oh no – it was definitely the linctus – the ambulance men had to wear masks when they carried her out!
MRS FITZ.	But however did it happen? Was she overcome by fumes?
MISS KING	They are a bit pungent if you rub too much on at a time.
MISS CLARE	No, she didn't rub it on – she drank it. (*Horror all round*) It tasted wonderful, she said – like Apricot Brandy and syrup of figs all mixed together. They got her to hospital only just in time.
MISS KING	You don't mean... she passed on?
MISS CLARE	No dear, just passed out. But she's going to be fine, once she can take solids again. But it was very nasty at the time – that Linctus ought to be banned, well at least properly labelled "not for human consumption".
MISS KING	HUMAN consumption?
MISS CLARE	Quite – it's for rubbing on dogs with kennel husk.
MISS KING	(*near to collapse*) But Dr John – he prescribes it for all his patients! Oh, how could he? He must KNOW what it's for!... I should have realised, he's trying to get rid of them all! Just so that he can play golf and improve his stupid handicap! I am so upset, I shall have to go home – poor Mrs Newnham... poor me! I shall never be able to look anyone in the face again! (*She goes out*)

CHRISTIE	I'd better give her a lift home; she'll never make it in that state. Let us know what you decide, Mrs. Downing – it's all the same to me. *(exit)*
MRS GIRTON	Good heavens, she's realised at last! Ah, well, there's not much point in hanging on – it's been nice to meet you, Miss Clare. Same time next week, Mrs Downing?
MRS DOWNING	Oh, yes Flora – thank you very much for coming. I really don't know WHAT we're going to do…
MRS FITZ	If it's alright with you, Mrs Downing, I'll just take these cups out and wash them up. Perhaps Flora would give me a hand, then we can leave together; I don't like going through the churchyard on my own – Silly really, and I know everyone there…
MRS GIRTON	You're an old fool, Emily… a NICE old fool! *(They go out together)*
MISS CLARE	Well, we seem to have come to rather an abrupt end, Mrs. Downing. But I really have enjoyed myself tremendously. Such a pleasant group of people – and quite a lot of talent hidden amongst the tangle of personalities. I shall be delighted to produce your Festival Play.
MRS DOWNING	But, Miss Clare… I'm very glad, of course, but – well, we haven't chosen a play yet – and you see how difficult it is. We could argue like this for weeks, and time is running out. It seems an impossible task.

MISS CLARE   As a matter of fact, I think I have the
              solution (*they rise and stand centre stage*) I
              rather like writing plays myself, and I have
              suddenly thought of such a good theme.
              Just imagine – the members of a Drama
              Group meet together to discuss the play
              they are going to put on for the
              forthcoming Drama Festival… (*they slowly
              leave the stage*) so they read various parts…
              (*the curtain is beginning to close*) but can't
              agree which one to do… (*they have left the
              stage, and the curtain closes*)

TIME BEING
– by Carol Reeve –

(This is in the form of a radio play, and can be performed on stage without the need for scenery or costumes)

CHARACTERS

Narrator

Fiona – about 25-30, a sensitive young widow

Sheila – z30-35, her sister, realistic, unmarried

Nancy – 55-60, their mother, vigorous and humorous

Jennie – 18, a sensible parlour maid

Georgina – 60-70, Victorian matron, supremely calm

Charlotte – 25, distraught and highly sensitive

NARRATOR	On the edge of a small village in Derbyshire, you may come across an old timbered cottage with long fingers of ivy shrouding the windows and encircling the chimney. The tiny garden is awash with dandelions. No one lives there now, but towards the end of Queen Victoria's reign it was the comfortable home of a much-respected elderly lady called Miss Georgina. She befriended her niece Charlotte, and they in turn were well looked after by their parlour maid, Jennie. The cottage is empty now - the For Sale sign has rotted away - and anyone enquiring in the village will be advised to stay well away - no-one has ventured beyond the broken front gate since... the accident. A few years ago, as darkness fell

one winter's evening, a small car swerved as it passed the cottage and crashed into a ditch. There were three ladies in the car, Nancy and her two grown-up daughters, Fiona and Sheila. It was Fiona who managed to stagger to the cottage first, and knocked urgently on the door.

FIONA
Hallo ? Hallo!-is there anyone at home?I say, can you help us… ? There's no-one in here either, Sheila. I wonder where they are. But what a gorgeous log fire! Look at this, Sheila!

SHEILA
That's something anyway - I'm absolutely frozen! What a strange place - it's almost like a museum! All those knick-knacks - and gas lamps! I thought electricity was laid on everywhere these days.

FIONA
Obviously not in the desolate wastes of Derbyshire. It must be at least ten miles since we passed a sizeable village.

SHEILA
More, I should say. I hope they've got a phone here - we shall need a break-down truck to get the car out of that ditch. Whatever came over you, Fiona? You're usually such a good driver.

FIONA
It was that damn cat - it seemed to appear from nowhere - it just stood in the road and flashed its great yellow eyes at me. It was - hypnotic. I had to force myself to swerve to avoid running over it. Have you got a cigarette, Sheila? I can't stop shaking.

SHEILA	Sorry - they're in my bag and that's still in the car. Poor old Fiona - no wonder we finished up in a ditch! Just for a moment you must have thought...
FIONA	Yes, I know what you were going to say. Just for a moment I thought it was all going to happen all over again... It's alright, Sheila, I don't mind talking about it. It's a help sometimes. Only last time Jim was driving. All I could do then was to sit there beside him and watch everything happen, wanting to reach out and grab the steering wheel, or the brake - anything - but in that split second of time I was paralysed with horror. Of course he was driving too fast - he should have run over the cat, and then we wouldn't have swerved into that oncoming car, and Jim wouldn't have been... he didn't stand a chance. I don't remember being pulled clear - but I can still see that black cat stalking away from the wreckage as though nothing had happened. Oh Sheila, how I hate black cats!
SHEILA	Poor darling!
FIONA	When I saw that cat just now, I really wanted to kill it, Sheila. And I tried! But I couldn't. Oh God, what a mess.
SHEILA	Oh, here's mother... we can't make anyone hear!

NANCY — I've looked everywhere, but the place seems deserted - just like the Marie Celeste! There's something cooking in a pan on a real old-fashioned range in the kitchen, and there are two places laid in the dining room. I suppose they are all upstairs, though you'd think they would have heard us and come down by now.

FIONA — We haven't been exactly quiet - we could be burglars!

SHEILA — Perhaps they like burglars - it might explain why they left the front door unlocked.. It's all very strange. Have you noticed, mother? No electric lights, not even a tele! But this log fire is really marvellous. It not only looks friendly, it smells so good. Reminds me of Father Christmas and hot buttered toast.

NANCY — Well, here's your toasting fork - all we need is a thick wedge of cottage loaf and some home-churned butter…

FIONA — Oh Mother, don't! I'm starving, aren't you?

NANCY — Yes, that meal we had in Buxton was very good, but even mountains of curry and rice can dwindle into misty memory after a few hours. If Fiona hadn't insisted on exploring every twisting country lane and kept to the main roads, we might have been tucking into egg and chips now! – instead of licking our wounds in this Victorian mausoleum in the middle of nowhere. At least we can keep warm while we wait for someone to materialise.

NARRATOR	They sit down by the fire, warming themselves. After a moment, the door opens, and JENNIE the maid comes in. The visitors stand, but Jennie moves between them and goes to the fire, where she puts on a log from the bin. Then she moves to the chairs and straightens the antimacassars. All the while, NANCY is talking to her, and does not notice when Miss Georgina enters the room.
NANCY	We're sorry to intrude like this, but you didn't hear us when we called. We've crashed our car in the lane, and we wondered if we could use your phone?
GEORGINA	Miss Charlotte will be down in a moment, Jennie. You may serve dinner in ten minutes.
JENNIE	Very good, Madam.
GEORGINA	… and draw the curtains, will you Jennie? It seems rather chilly in here this evening. I shall sit by the fire and do some more crochet work until dinner is ready.
NANCY	It is very kind of you to allow us in like this - we found the door open and couldn't make anyone hear.
SHEILA	We just wondered if we could use your phone…
NANCY	It's no good, Sheila - she can't hear us. Look at her face! She can't even see us! I'll flash my hand in front of her face - just watch what happens… There, you see? No reaction at all.
FIONA	She must be blind.

NANCY	AND deaf? No: as far as she is concerned, we are just not here.
SHEILA	But that's impossible!
NANCY	I wonder if this will convince you!
NARRATOR	Nancy walks over to the fireplace and picks up the toasting fork. She raises it above her head and makes as if to strike the old lady. Georgina goes on working her crochet
FIONA	Mother, that was an awful thing to do!
NANCY	Maybe, but it proves my point. I've read about things like this – but I never really believed it till now. It's rather exciting! Look – the little maid has come back!
JENNIE	I'm worried about Miss Charlotte, Madam. She's gone out into the lane without her cloak. Shall I go and fetch her?
GEORGINA	Oh that poor dear girl! I had hoped that after three months with us she would have found the strength to fight these moments of desolation. Be patient with her, Jennie. Her young spirit has been crushed and scattered, and until the horror of that dreadful accident begins to fade, we cannot help her. To lose one's family in such terrible circumstances - father, mother and brother - all perished together - that is too much for any child to bear.
JENNIE	How did it happen, Madam?

GEORGINA	Fire, Jennie. It was thought a spark from a chimney fire set alight the timbers in the roof, and the old house blazed up before anyone could be saved. Miss Charlotte was away in Cheshire, staying with friends, and somehow she feels that if only she had been at home, the tragedy might not have happened... its nonsense, of course, but in her poor shattered mind there is no place for reason. We must be patient, Jennie, and pray for her.
JENNIE	Yes, Madam, I understand. Shall I bring her in now?
GEORGINA	Thank you.
FIONA	Oh God, this is awful. It's like a nightmare.
SHEILA	Let's get out of here, Mother.
NANCY	Fascinating, isn't it? I've always wanted to meet a ghost. The amazing thing is that I don't feel at all frightened.
FIONA	Oh Mother! Speak for yourself! For heavens sake let's get out.
NANCY	Where to? It was your idea to cut across country to get away from the main roads - goodness knows where the next village is, and it must be dark outside now. At least we can be warm here - and there's plenty to eat in the kitchen...
SHEILA	But we can't just help ourselves... I mean, it doesn't seem right !

NANCY	Why not? Don't you realise what these people are? They are ghosts, shades from a past century. We can't disturb them anymore than they can disturb us!
FIONA	Mother, what are you saying? How can you be so... so dispassionate? You call them ghosts - I call them dead souls.
NANCY	Of course they are - dead in OUR time, but not in theirs. That's what makes it so wonderful... surely this is a rare vision of eternal life!
SHEILA	Now you are being ridiculous. This house is haunted, that's all, and the sooner we get out the better.
FIONA	I think we must all be suffering from concussion and imagining it all.
NANCY	This fire is real enough, isn't it? The moment we entered that door we stepped back a hundred years or so - just wait till I tell my Guild members! We must have inadvertently crossed some Time barrier...
SHEILA	Oh, I've no patience with you, Mother- you watch too much television. The whole thing is beyond understanding. Sh! Someone is coming!
CHARLOTTE	I'm sorry I've been so long, Aunt. I thought I heard Blackie crying in the lane: I called and called but he didn't come.
GEORGINA	Oh my poor love. Blackie went away three weeks ago, but you cannot accept that he will not return. Jennie could bring you a kitten from the farm. Would you like that?
CHARLOTTE	He will come back, I know he will...

GEORGINA	Yes, dear. Come and sit by the fire. Jennie will be serving dinner shortly.
FIONA	That cat in the lane… it must have been a ghost too! A black shadow from the past…
SHEILA	I've got goose pimples all over! Can't we just go, Mother, and leave them alone?
FIONA	How serene they are - so remote and yet so alive. I wonder if we could touch them…
NARRATOR	And Fiona gently touches Charlotte on the shoulder.
CHARLOTTE	Oh… I thought for a moment… there must be a draught somewhere. Do you feel cold, Aunt?
GEORGINA	No dear. But there is a strange chilliness in here this evening. Perhaps the wind is coming from the north.
SHEILA	You see? They can SENSE we are here - we're intruding into their lives.
NANCY	Nonsense. You look awful, Fiona. That crash must have upset you more than we know. Sheila, go and fetch the luggage from the car. There's nowhere else to go, and perhaps we can get a little sleep by the fire when these spirits have gone to bed. None of us will come to any harm if we just accept the situation and try not to fathom its mysteries.
SHEILA	Alright. I'll lock up the car, shall I? Not that anyone could drive it away.

NARRATOR   While Sheila is gone, Nancy examines the
                ornaments on the mantelpiece, and Fiona
                stares at Charlotte. Georgina works at her
                crochet. All at once, Charlotte lifts her
                head and looks straight at Fiona... and in
                that moment Time stands still.

FIONA   Can you see me, Charlotte? Perhaps you
                just feel that I am here. But you are not
                afraid, are you? How strange to feel such
                warmth for a ghost... because I do,
                Charlotte. You have suffered so much and
                I yearn to comfort you - somehow.
                Perhaps there is a way?... Once, not long
                ago, I loved someone very dearly and he
                was taken from me, and no amount of
                sympathetic words could fill the emptiness
                that overwhelmed me. But slowly, very
                slowly, the wound healed, and left a scar
                which aches sometimes, just to remind me
                what might have been... You mustn't
                blame yourself, Charlotte... try to believe
                that your life has a new purpose now: to
                fulfill the dreams and desires that your
                loved ones would have wished for you. Be
                strong - step out of the darkness and into
                the sunshine, where there is life, and hope,
                and love. Do you hear me, Charlotte? Yes,
                I se that you do. Reach out and touch my
                hand, Charlotte - compassion will
                transcend Time.

NARRATOR   In the silent stillness of that moment, the
                girls reach out and their hands touch.
                Then Charlotte withdraws her hand and
                shivers a little. She kneels beside her Aunt.

CHARLOTTE   Aunt, have you ever...

GEORGINA   What, dear?

CHARLOTTE   Oh, its nothing. It's just that… for a
                moment it seemed that something or
                someone had lifted up my heart and
                brushed away my sorrow…

GEORGINA   My dear - what a strange thing to say!

CHARLOTTE   Yes, I suppose it was. But yet I feel… look
                at me Aunt! Have I not changed?

GEORGINA   Well, it is true that there is a new
                brightness in your eyes - and you smile as I
                have not seen you smile since…

CHARLOTTE   Yes, Aunt - since I came to make my home
                with you. Oh Aunt - how good you are to
                me!

NARRATOR   As she buries her head in her Aunt's lap
                and weeps for the first time, Sheila runs
                into the room, her face pale and her eyes
                wide.

SHEILA   Mother … the car…

NANCY   Why, what's happened?

SHEILA   It's there alright, all smashed up, just as we
                left it. But when I looked inside,I could
                see… Oh, my God…

FIONA   What did you see, Sheila?

SHEILA   Inside I could see three people… just lying
                there… quite still… So I opened the
                door… and Fiona, the one in the driving
                seat was you! And lying beside you, with
                her eyes staring up at me, was Mother -
                and I knew before I looked that the one in
                the back was me…

NANCY	But that's impossible - we're all here!
SHEILA	I swear to you…
FIONA	No, it's true. Our bodies are out there. I knew it somehow, it just didn't make sense…
GEORGINA	Shall we go into dinner, dear?
FIONA	… but now I understand.
CHARLOTTE	Yes, Aunt. Shall I take your wrap?
SHEILA	Who are the ghosts now?
NANCY	Don't go, Charlotte - stay with us!
FIONA	It is time for us to leave - are you coming, Sheila?
SHEILA	Yes, I'm ready.
NANCY	But where to? Where are we going?
FIONA	Does it matter? We have to go - somewhere. We have done what we came to do, and now we must go. We do not belong to this time.
JENNIE	Miss Charlotte, you'll never guess what's happened!
FIONA	Come Mother - Sheila - it is time to go… time… Time…
CHARLOTTE	Why, what is it. Jennie?
JENNIE	It's Blackie, Miss! He's come home! He's dirty and frightened, but he's in the kitchen now, lapping from his saucer of milk as though he'd only been out for a few hours!

CHARLOTTE   Oh Jennie - Aunt! There, I said he'd come back! You see, Aunt , suddenly everything has changed, as though a great shadow had crossed our lives. But now the sun is pouring through the windows and turning winter into spring. How happy I am!

NARRATOR   As Georgina prepares to follow Charlotte and Jennie into dinner, she turns and picks up the toasting fork . She puzzles over it, and then replaces it quietly in its proper place. She looks around the room, and then appears to be listening - she shivers and leaves the room. Outside, Fiona's voice drifts away into the night...

FIONA   ... it is time... time... time

KEEP FIT CLASS,
– by Carol Reeve –

A very short play for 6 women and one man

CHARACTERS
    Mrs. Phyllis Watson
    Her friend, Elsie,
    Petunia
    Miss Floyd
    Arnold Twiggett
    Mrs. Bloggs
    Jane

(The curtains open on an apparently empty stage, but as the lights go up, a figure is just discernible asleep in a corner. Voices are heard off stage)

ELSIE   I expect we're first as usual.

PHYLLIS   Never mind, we can have a quick fag, dear.

(They enter, a homely pair, middle aged. Phyllis is the Oliver Hardy to Elsie's Stan Laurel. Phyllis takes out a packet of fags and they light up.)

PHYLLIS   Phew, that's better. Keep a lookout for
                 Miss Floyd., Elsie - you know how a whiff
                 of woodbines gives her the vapours.

(Elsie peers out between flats)

ELSIE   Cant see her yet, Phyllis. *(she turns to her)*
               She's right, really, you know. Smoking
               never did anyone any good.

PHYLLIS   Oh yes it did, dear - me! I gave it up once,
               when our Willie was saving for that drum-
               kit, and within three days I'd put on nearly
               half a stone. Couldn't stop nibbling,
                 biscuits, toffees, carrots, anything - my
               mouth used to ache every time I passed a
               cake shop. The sight of that lovely gooey
               cream oozing out of those delicious
               chocolate-covered éclairs…

ELSIE   Oh stop it Phyllis, I can't bear it!

PHYLLIS   Well, I just had to give up giving up
               smoking - now if I feel like a little nibble I
               pick up the ashtrays and sniff at the fag-
               ends.

ELSIE   Ooh Phyllis, you are awful! The others are
               late, aren't they?

PHYLLIS   Well, Mrs. Smithers has taken their Reggie
               to the dentist, so she wont be coming. And
               the Peabody sisters are playing hockey -
               and Mrs. Higgins's husband's aunt has just
               arrived from Brazil - but I expect Mrs.
               Bloggs'll turn up as usual.

ELSIE   Oh, yes, she'd never miss a class. Do you
               remember that time she sprained her ankle
               rescuing a tortoise from the top of an oak
               tree?

PHYLLIS   *(Patiently)* Tortoise SHELL, dear - tortoise
               shell CAT.

ELSIE   Oh, yes. Well, she struggled along here for
                    the Keep Fit Class. Couldn't join in, of
                    course, but I think she only comes for the
                    company. Leads a lonely life.

*(Petunia enters. She is languid and luscious. She saunters to centre
stage, and relaxes on one hip. The others survey her with scorn)*

PHYLLIS   *(aside)* Don't know why that one bothers
                    to come - unless its to show up the rest of
                    us.

ELSIE   Now, don't be like that, Phyllis. I think
                    she's lovely.

PHYLLIS   *(aside)* So does she! *(To Petunia)* Turned
                    out nice again, hasn't it?

PETUNIA   S'pose so. *(She changes to other hip)*

PHYLLIS   *(mimicking)* S'pose so! Lives in a dream,
                    that one. If you told her the place was
                    burning down, I expect she'd say "s'pose
                    so" Well, better loosen up a bit.

*(Phyllis stretches out her arms and twists a bit, then reached down
to touch the floor, at least a yard out)*

PHYLLIS   Cor, Elsie, I knew I shouldn't have had
                    that second dumpling at dinner-time.

ELSIE   Dumpling? Oh, Phyllis, you really
                    shouldn't. I haven't touched anything
                    fattening for weeks. Hasn't been easy
                    though. I have to close my eyes when I
                    give Arthur his roly-poly.

PHYLLIS   *(mischievously)* I bet he enjoys that!

ELSIE   *(all innocent)* Oh he does. Sometimes twice
                    a week - and he always has a second
                    helping.

(Phyllis cries out with mirth, to Elsie's amazement. Just then MISS Floyd enters, hard as nails)

MISS L	Have I missed something, Mrs. Watson?
PHYLLIS	I wouldn't be at all surprised. *(she collapses again with mirth. Miss Floyd is not at all amused.)*
MISS F	Bit late, I'm afraid - Mother caught her nightie in the lawnmower. Well, let's get started.
ELSIE	Mrs. Bloggs hasn't come yet.
MISS F	Mrs. Bloggs? Of course she has. I saw her just now. She's over there.

(They all look at the sleeping figure, and Phyllis goes over to wake her)

PHYLLIS	Wake up, dearie. Class is about to start.

(Mrs. Bloggs blinks and staggers to her feet)

MRS B	Start? Oh thank goodness! I thought I'd missed it all again.
ELSIE	We never saw you come in, dear. My, your clothes are all bedraggled - you look as though you've been sleeping there all week... *(sudden possibility dawns, and Phyllis and Elsie look at each other in horror)*
PHYLLIS	Never! Someone would have noticed...
ELSIE	Well, she lives all alone- the neighbours might have thought she'd gone to her daughter's for a few days...
PHYLLIS	Oh my goodness! *(To Mrs. Bloggs)* How are you feeling now, dear? A bit peckish I shouldn't wonder?

MRS. BLOGGS	No - no- a bit stiff perhaps. And I'll have to visit the little girl's room before we start.
PHYLLIS	I should think so too - don't know how you've hung on so long!
MISS FLOYD	Really, Mrs Watson! Such impertinence!
PHYLLIS	But she's been here all week...
MRS B	Nonsense, dear, what an idea! Got here a bit early, that's all. Felt a bit faint in the Library. Can't think why they don't put the titles facing the same way on the shelves - its like watching tennis in a flea circus... *(she demonstrates, and exits)*
MISS F.	Now come along, ladies. The Camera Club will be here soon and we don't want to be caught in the middle of our plies.

(They line up facing the audience, Miss F to one side)

ELSIE	Shouldn't we wait for Mrs. Bloggs?
PHYLLIS	She won't be back yet, dear - you know her, in for a penny, in for...
MISS F	Now that's enough. *(puts on record)* Arms up - and forward - swing down and touch your toes - and UP - and forward... *(etc. etc. This should be carefully rehearsed to precision and dead-pan faces)*
MISS F	Sideways BEND and bend and UP - other side - bend and bend and UP, and TURN *(they are now backs to the audience, and go down, legs apart, to touch floor)*
MISS F	... and HOLD it... *(just then a little man enters shyly down front)*

MAN   Excuse me, am I too late?

(There is a moments hush - then the ladies recover quickly and turn to stare at the intruder)

MAN   This is the Camera Club, isn't it?

MISS F   Certainly not. This is the Ladies' Keep Fit Class.

MAN   I am most tewwibly sowwy… they asked me to come early to get my thlide projector thet up. I'm giving a lecture on the Beautiful Beaches of Bwitain.

(Something strange has happened to Miss Floyd. She is staring at the intruder, mouth open)

MISS F   Arnold! Arnold Twiggett… it must be! After all these years!

PHYLLIS   Oh Gawd!

ARNOLD   I'm thorry, I don't… my name ITH Arnold Twiggett, but I can't quite…

MISS F   Don't you remember? Flora Floyd, Brighton 1982! *(He looks at her speechless, then recovers)*

ARNOLD   Flora Floyd! Why, yeth! Flora! Of courth! You haven't changed a bit!

(She goes all coy and demure, mush to the fascination of Phyllis and Elsie)

MISS F   Neither have you, Arnold! Do you remember how we used to sit at the end of the Pier under your umbrella?

PHYLLIS   *(aside)* Cosy!

MISS F	… and how you wrote our names in the sand with little round pebbles… and that naughty doggie who ate up your sandwiches while you were flying your kite…
PHYLLIS	Whatever next?!
MISS F	Seeing you again like this has unlocked the most precious of long-forgotten memories… *(she hooks her arm through his and leads him to one side)*
PHYLLIS	You wouldn't believe it possible, would you Elsie? She'll swallow him whole in a minute, just you wait and see.
ELSIE	I think its lovely, so romantic. Don't you, Petunia?
PETUNIA	S'pose so.
PHYLLIS.	Might as well have a sit down while they relive the swinging sixties.

(While they settle on the edge of the stage, legs dangling, Flora is teasing Arnold in the corner - he is presumably overcome at the situation)

PHYLLIS	Got a lovely bit of steak this morning, Elsie. Going to smother it with mushrooms and chips and you see if our Willie doesn't buy me that new hat tomorrow!
ELSIE	Oh you are awful, Phyllis. Whatever do you want a new hat for?
PHYLLIS	To go with that pink dress and the fur coat and the crocodile handbag and shoes that I've seen in Harringes.

ELSIE	But your Willie will never agree to all that?
PHYLLIS	He'll have to! Got to have something to go with my new hat.

(Some altercation is going on in the corner)

MISS F	But you said twelve o'clock, and I waited for an hour in the rain and you never came…
ARNOLD	One o'clock, Flora, one o'clock. You didn't turn up and I had to catch my twain…
FLORA	Never a word, not a single line. You broke my heart , Arnold.
ARNOLD	*(embarrassed)* There, there, Flora - don't upthet yourself!

(He takes out his handkerchief and is mopping her eyes when Mrs. Bloggs re-enters.)

MRS. B	I do believe I must have dropped off for a bit.
PHYLLIS	You haven't missed much, dear. Just the balcony scene from Romeo and Juliet.

(Arnold is transfixed, staring at Mrs. Bloggs. She sees him and goes closer in her short-sighted way)

MRS. B	Funny - seeing you standing there, you reminded me of that undernourished young man who jilted my daughter way back in 1983, while we were on holiday in Southport… now, what was his name?
PHYLLIS	Wouldn't be Arnold Twiggett, by any chance?

MRS B	Why yes! However did you guess? It WAS Arnold Twiggett... Just a minute... *(she goes closer and he backs away, mopping his brow)*
MRS B	It IS you, isn't it? It all comes back to me now ... Dolores told me how you used to sit on the Pier in all weathers, cuddling up under his umbrella...
MISS F	Oh no!
MRS B	... and picking out your names with little pebbles on the beach...
MISS F	I can't bear it! You ... you... Casanova you!
PHYLLIS	How about flying his kite, Mrs. Bloggs?
MRS B	I don't remember that. But he was too mean to take her into a café - always had sandwiches on the beach...

(Miss Floyd is overcome, but bearing up well)

MISS F	You... gigolo, Arnold Twiggett - how many more poor girls are there up and down the country waiting for you to fulfil your empty promises? A broken heart bleeding on every beach in Britain..
ELSIE	Oh Miss Floyd! *(she is near to tears)*
MRS. B	There was my Dolores, waiting for hours in the rain for you to turn up. "You're better off without him" I told her - mean as mustard, and twice as crafty you are, Arnold Twiggett.
MISS F	Two-faced, deceitful, unscrupulous...

(He is between them the picture of dejection. Unseen by all, a little sweet-faced woman has entered the stage. She sees Arnold and approaches hesitantly. She coughs. They pause in full flood).

JANE   Excuse me if I'm interrupting something. I've brought your sandwiches, Arnold - you left them on the kitchen table. And Tommy says will you mend his kite if you're not too late back home? And George says will you remember to bring him that book on geology from the library - and don't forget to pick up our Katie from the Brownies. Oh, and the twins left my umbrella at grandma's yesterday, if you could pop in there? I'm off to Bingo now - oh, and baby 's bottle is all ready for his ten o'clock feed. Can you remember all that, dear?

(There is a numbed silence - Arnold recovers first)

ARNOLD   Yeth, yeth dear - but, hang on a minute and I'll thee you to the bus... I've dethided not to give the lecture thith evening... my-my pwojector's not focuthing too well...
(he bustles her out and they exit)

PHYLLIS   Well, what a turn-up! From philanderer to father of five in a flash!

ELSIE   I think it was six, Phyllis.

PHYLLIS   Anyhow, our Miss Floyd and Mrs. Blogg's
               daughter are well rid of him. Talk about
               wolf in sheep's clothing!

MRS. B   You're right, Phyllis - my Dolores had a
               narrow escape there - to think she might
               have been a down-trodden mother of six
               now, instead of a manicurist in a Poodle
               Parlour.

PHYLLIS   Yes, it's a dog's life whichever way you
               look at it.

ELSIE   Oh Phyllis, you are awful!

(Miss Floyd has recovered her former composure)

MISS F   Now that's enough frivolity. We've had a
               very unpleasant interlude, but its all over
               now. Next week I shall expect you all here
               a quarter of an hour early to make up for
               the valuable time lost today. You may go
               now.

*(Mrs B, Phyllis and Elsie collect their things. As they prepare to
go, Elsie goes up to Miss Floyd and puts out her hand to touch her
sympathetically on the arm, but Phyllis pulls her away. As they
reach the side, Phyllis turns)*

PHYLLIS   Are you coming, Petunia?

PETUNIA   S'pose so.

*(She meanders off. Miss Faggott is alone. She picks up her bag,
then turns and stands for a minute centre stage.*

MISS F   *(softly)* Arnold Twiggett... Oh, Arnold!
               *(Then briskly she strides off, and the play is
               over.)*

Carol Reeve

STATELY SUNFLOWERS
– by Carol Reeve –

CHARACTERS
   Lily-Ann – an American Tourist
   Petunia – her friend
   Grandma Clegg
   Mum Clegg
   Julia Clegg – daughter
   Susan Clegg
   A Thief
   A Detective
   A Cleaning lady

Scene: A Stately Home. The Guide enters, followed by all the tourists. The Americans are at her heels, panting but enthusiastic. The Cleggs struggle in afterwards, the children last.)

GUIDE	...and finally, this is the Blue Drawing Room, the last of the 305 rooms on our guided tour of Hockley Hall.
GRANDMA	Seems more like 500... oh! My poor feet... Susan! Don't touch that goblet!
GUIDE	As you can see, there is an old master hanging on every wall in this room...
JULIA	Cor! This could be just the place for old Pussy-foot!
MUM	Julia! Show respect for your teacher... and "Mr Moggins" if you please.

SUSAN	*(to Julia)* Yes – he'd just about fit in between that man with his ear all bandaged and that one with a silly hat and a lace collar.
GUIDE	As the young lady has noted, here we have Van Gogh's self portrait and the famous Franz Hals' Laughing Cavalier.
LILY-ANN	Do you hear that, Petunia? That is the famous Van Goge picture when he'd just cut off his ear! Isn't that amazing?
PETUNIA	That is truly amazing!
JULIA	Why did he cut his ear off?
LILY-ANN	I beg your pardon, honey?
JULIA	I said why did he cut off his ear?
LILY-ANN	Well, I don't rightly know. Do you know, Miss –er – Mrs Guide?
GUIDE	I understand that Mr Van GOFF removed his ear because he was annoyed with his friend Gauguin.
GRANDMA-	By gum, that were a stupid prank.
SUSAN	He should have cut off his friend's ear! I would've!
MUM	*(smacking her)* You keep your opinions to yourself, young lady!

(Thief creeps in, looks slowly round at the pictures)

GUIDE	Then he sent his ear to his friend in a parcel. *(Girls: UGH!!)*
LILY-ANN	Fancy that, Petunia! And then sitting down and painting his own face, bandages and all!

PETUNIA	Isn't that amazing, Lily-Ann?
GUIDE	And over on the south wall you will see the famous painting know as the Haywain.
MUM	I know who painted that! It were *(she turns and faces the Thief)* Constable!

(The Thief gives a quiet scream and puts her hands in the air.)

GRANDMA	So it were, luv. John Constable. *(Thief retreats and gathers her breath)* We used to have a postcard with that on – my mother kept it on her mantelpiece for years. It covered up a damp patch on the wallpaper until the patch grew bigger than the postcard.

(The plain-clothes cop/detective now enters. It is very obvious that she is tailing the Thief.)

LILY-ANN	*(To Guide)* Tell me, Mrs Guide. How come there are so many famous masterpieces all gathered together in this one room?
GUIDE	Well, Madam, the last Lord Hockley made his fortune in tin foil, especially in the manufacture of foil lifts…
LILY-ANN	*(to Petunia)* "Elevators", honey… *(She nods)*
GUIDE	But unfortunately the bottom dropped out of the market. However, by that time he had acquired this incredible collection from big galleries around the country. He also bought several statues – some Henry Moore's and Epstein's.
SUSAN	What's that one over there? *(pointing to Detective who has a lampshade over her head and is not breathing.)*

GRANDMA   Looks like a standard lamp to me!

(Thief wanders over and touches lampshade. Detective's eyes go up to ceiling… Thief wanders off again.)

MUM   Probably one of them pre-rufflette tape jobs.

GRANDMA   Rufflette tapes? Why are you going on about curtains all of a sudden?

MUM;-   Curtains? I never mentioned curtains!

GRANDMA-   Yes, you did. You were on about rufflette tape jobs.

MUM   No! No! PRE-rufflette tape – Rosetti, Dante, Gabriel, you know, that lot!

GRANDMA-   No, I don't know. You're talking rubbish.

MUM   Oh, do be quiet, Mother – you're showing your ignorance again.

GRANDMA-   *(anxiously looking down at her hem)* Oh dear, am I?

GUIDE   Excuse me, madam, but I couldn't help overhearing. I believe your daughter was referring to the Pre-Raphaelites…

MUM-   That's what I said – pre-rufflette tapes.

JULIA; -   Mum!

MUM   Now what is it?

JULIA   That's not a standard lamp – it's someone holding a lampshade over her head. Look! *(They turn, but the shade is now on a table, and the detective has vanished behind a curtain)*

MUM   *(cuffing Julia)* Honestly, Julia, you get more like your father every day! Stupid, lazy AND a liar!

GUIDE	Ladies , may I draw your attention to the prize possession in this room – a recent acquisition I might add – over there you will see the famous "Sunflowers" by Vincent Van Gogh. *(They all admire the picture)*
PETUNIA	Isn't that amazing, Lily-Ann?
LILY-ANN	Sure is, . It's –er – a trifle smaller than I imagined.
GUIDE	Yes, most of our visitors express surprise – and I might say doubts. However, the explanation is simple enough. This was the original study of sunflowers painted by Van Gogh. The one recently bought by the National Gallery is a late copy.
LILY-ANN	Gee – do they know they spent millions on a copy?
GUIDE	*(affronted)* But of course, Madam! A copy is not the same as a forgery, - not when the original painter copied his own work.
LILY-ANN	Sounds funny to me – gee, if they spent millions on a copy, what must that one be worth?
GUIDE	Ah – impossible to speculate! It's virtually priceless… priceless!
PETUNIA	Why, that is amazing, is it not, Lily-Ann?

(As they all gaze in wonder, the thief turns to the audience and shows her glee, with a wink and thumbs up . Enter Cleaning lady, with bucket and mop)

CLEANER   Come on, you lot, it's five o'clock and the
                 doors are bein' bolted downstairs. Get a
                 move on – I want to get finished in good
                 time tonight.

GUIDE   Ah – come along then, ladies. If you would
                 like to make your way out by the back
                 stairs over there… *(She shows the way, and
                 stands with her hand out, waiting for tips, but
                 nothing, just a handshake for Lily-Ann. Guide
                 shrugs and exits, leaving the cleaner alone. The
                 detective is behind the curtain. She sings as she
                 cleans. The Thief re-enters, goes up to the
                 Sunflowers, and tucks it under her mac.
                 Detective runs out and grabs her)*

DETECTIVE   Got you at last, Cristabel Creep! I arrest
                 you, in the name of the law.

CLEANER   'Ere, what's goin' on? You'll be knockin'
                 me Meissen off of me Chippendale if
                 you're not careful!

DETECTIVE   I am Detective Constable P-P-P- Pinge,
                 and I am nicking this villain for p-p-p-
                 purloining this p-p-p-painting!

CLEANER   What painting? Cor! Give it 'ere! *(She takes
                 Sunflowers and dusts it lovingly)* That's one of
                 me favourites! Ere, how dare you come in
                 'ere, thievin' and arrestin' and messin' up
                 me carpets? Off with the both of you,
                 before I clock you wiv me bucket!

(They go off in a hurry, detective collaring the thief)

CLEANER   *(to picture)* There now, poor old
                 Sunflowers. That nasty woman has made
                 your petals all grimy. Never mind. We'll
                 soon put that to rights.

(As she bends to get things out of her bucket, the twins reappear and stand out of her sight. Cleaner takes palette, and oil paint brush out of her bucket, and begins to touch up Sunflowers.)

CLEANER   There, that's better! Good as new! How about the rest of you – your hat looks

                       very shabby, Cavalier – a bit more black on there, I think… and we'll have to do something about those rusty wheels on the Haywain…

(The twins are horrified)

JULIA   But you can't do that ! You'll ruin them!

SUSAN   They're worth millions!

CLEANER   *(startled)* Cor stone the crows! You didn't half give me a fright! What are you doing here anyway? The last tour left ages ago.

JULIA   It's HER fault – we were looking for the loo and got lost in the corridors.

SUSAN   No it wasn't ! It was YOUR fault. You took us the wrong way.

CLEANER   Never mind – never mind! If you go through that door and down the stairs, the guide will still be 'anging around the 'all.

JULIA   We saw you – vandalising the pictures!

CLEANER   *(Nearly speechless)* Vandalisin'! Vandalisin'! 'Ow dare you! Touchin' up maybe, or improvin' the finish more like… I'll 'ave you know. I never let one of me pictures get dirty or flaky like those other nasty things what used to be 'ung up 'ere.

SUSAN   What "other nasty things"?

- 81 -

CLEANER	Them pictures wot Lord Hockley had put up – never saw such a faded lot of old paintings. Of course, I 'ad a go at cleanin' 'em wiv Swarfega – then I 'ad to patch 'em up a bit wiv my nephew's paint box, and found I was quite good at it!
JULIA	You mean you painted over all the original masterpieces?
CLEANER	That's right.
SUSAN	So aren't these the originals with your patching all over them?
CLEANER	No! In the end I decided to do a proper job, so I copied 'em all! I painted 'em onto some old wallpaper samples, and then put 'em into the big old picture frames.
JULIA	So what happened to the originals then?
CLEANER	Oh, I took 'em down to a car boot sale behind the Vernon Arms and sold 'em all for a fiver.
SUSAN	Crikey! Didn't anyone suspect?
CLEANER	No. They all looked a bit tatty by then, after my scrubbin' 'em, and no-one noticed 'ere because I'd made such a good job of my copies. Not bad, are they?
JULIA	I think they're terrific!
SUSAN	What about that one – the Sunflowers? The guide said it was a recent acqui… acqui…
JULIA	… sition, silly.

CLEANER

Tricky, that was – I copied it from the REAL one – you know, in the National Gallery. Then the present Lord Hockley caught me carrying it into the Blue Room,- so on the spur of the moment I said I'd just found it in the attic!

JULIA

And he believed you?

CLEANER

Daft, isn't he? He was as pleased as Punch! Still – can't blame him really – Who would ever imagine a cleaning lady being capable of turnin' out artistic replications like that?

SUSAN

Of course – no-one would! You're brilliant!

CLEANER

Thanks, dearie. Seein' as you're bein' so understandin', I'll let you into a little secret. I'm half-way through the Mona Lisa!

JULIA

Cor! Another discovery in the attic?

(They all laugh)

CLEANER

I suppose it will 'ave to be! And after that I wouldn't mind 'avin' a go at a Goya!

(Voices off,

Mum and Grandma "Where are you? Susan? Julia! Where've you got to?"

CLEANER

Run along now – and mind! Not a word to no-one – right?

GIRLS TOGETHER Right!

CLEANER

Right!!

(The twins run off, calling. Cleaner is left alone with her pictures.)

CLEANER   Time I was movin' on too – got to do the
                 Long Gallery and the Conservatory yet.
                 And while I'm about it, I must remember
                 to have another go at gluein' that Ming
                 vase I broke yesterday – should look like
                 new with a bit of Superglue. Ah well – it's
                 just one Ming after another! Ta-ra, me
                 lovelies, ta-ra! *(Exit)*

COMMITTEE MEETING

– by Carol Reeve –

CAST

> Mrs. Roberts – the Vicar's wife,
> Mrs Boles – Guide captain
> Miss Small – Committee secretary
> Mrs. Webb – greengrocer's wife
> Lady Spooner – wife of the local Squire

ROBERTS	I hope Lady Spooner will not be late.
BOLES;	So do I – I have a Guide meeting at six.
SMALL	I put 4.30 on her Minutes, and I underlined it. I hope it didn't offend her Ladyship! It's past five now.
WEBB	You shouldn't be so scared of her, Miss Small. Don't you stand for any of her overbearing ways.
ROBERTS	She is a customer of yours I believe, Mrs Webb?
WEBB	She is that – and I always sell her good honest fresh veggies. She can't quarrel with me for that. No reason at all. But she does!
BOLES	I always tell my Guides…
SMALL	Hush – here she is! *(Lady Spooner sweeps in)*
SPOONER	Well, here we are, and nobody late. Now then let's make a start – no good wasting time.

SMALL	Here are the Minutes of the last Meeting, your Ladyship.
SPOONER	*(sweeping book off the table)* The last meeting was about the smell from the piggeries. This is about the Garden Fete. No need whatsoever to read all that nonsense. Now, it will be held in my garden as usual.
ROBERTS	The Vicar said he thought we could perhaps have it this year in the Vicarage garden…
SPOONER	In my garden as usual. Now, as to the date…
BOLES	The Guide rally is…
SPOONER	July 25th suits me best.
ROBERTS	Oh – but that is the Saturday the Vicar is away, Lady Spooner.
SPOONER	He will have to go away another day.
SMALL	Why not the Saturday after, your Ladyship?
WEBB	P'raps I shouldn't butt in, so to speak, but Saturday the 25th is the Baptist's bunfight.
SPOONER	Is that supposed to thrill me, Mrs Webb?
SMALL	The first of August would be better really, your Ladyship.
SPOONER	I have people coming to stay that day and I cannot have the garden full of riff-raff.
ROBERTS	Then lets hold it in the Vicarage garden.
SPOONER	It has already been settled where it is to be held. If everyone would attend properly there would not be all this muddle.

WEBB	I am one as likes to speak 'er mind…
SPOONER	I am sure that is very praiseworthy, Mrs Webb, but hardly a help when we are discussing the Garden Fete.
ROBERTS	Then it's agreed we have it on August the first.
SPOONER	July 25th you mean.
ROBERTS	But the Vicar…
BOLES	The Guides cannot possibly attend two events.
SMALL	Miss Styles the headmistress sent word to say the school children have prepared an entertainment.
SPOONER	I cannot agree to that. I will not have that horde of children running wild.
WEBB	My Harold were there last year and he never run wild, I'll take my oath on it.
SPOONER	Then he wasn't there, Mrs Webb, as ALL the children last year ran wild and ruined my borders, so my gardener tells me.
ROBERTS	But the parents all come, and it brings lots of money.
SMALL	Miss Styles is very anxious…
BOLES	The Guides could look after the borders if the date was altered.
SMALL	Is the date decided, then?
SPOONER	All this discussion seems very unnecessary.

WEBB	It's worse than the smell from the piggeries. We're not getting nowhere, and we didn't then- the smell's as bad as ever. It takes more than a Meeting to stop them pigs smelling.
SMALL	Mrs, Webb – please! What am I to say to Miss Styles, your Ladyship?
ROBERTS	Oh, do lets have the children, Lady Spooner. They dance so prettily!
WEBB	My Harold's in it.
SPOONER	Do you have last year's list of stallholders, Miss Small? Just see all those people and tell them to arrange the same stalls as before. But no ice-cream van this year . Creates such a mess. My gardener will arrange the bowling and the clock golf, and the Bishop will open the Fete.
ROBERTS	We've had the Bishop eleven times, Lady Spooner.
WEBB	He's no treat to nobody now, and he never buys nowt. Except in the beer tent…
BOLES	What about Mrs Ashmore, the Commissioner? The Guides…
SPOONER	The Bishop can only manage the 25th.
ROBERTS	But I thought we'd agreed on August the first!

SPOONER   Well, that concludes the Meeting I think...
             Now, is everything quite clear? July 25th,
             no children dancing, no ice-cream van,
             and the Bishop will open it. I am sure we
             have held a very agreeable Meeting and
             everything amicably settled. Good
             afternoon, everyone.

*(She sweeps out. The members look at each other, shrug their
shoulders and say:)*

ALL   I don't know why we bother to come.
             (Exeunt)

Carol Reeve

SKETCHES

Carol Reeve

SNOW WHITE AND THE WICKED QUEEN

– by Carol Reeve –

CHARACTERS
    Compere
    Snow White
    The Queen.

COMPERE	Good evening, all. Now it is time
	For you to see our pantomime.
	Unfortunately, due to 'flu,
	Our cast of thousand's down to two…
	But we'll endeavour, none the less,
	To do our play with eagerness.
	Our little play will be quite masterly…
	Although the rhymes are really ghasterly.
	Now hush! Behold - the curtains part
	Revealing Nature's works of art -
	Two lovely ladies: what a sight!
	The wicked Queen and poor Snow White.
QUEEN	I am the lovely, wicked Queen,
	The likes of me you've never seen…
	I gaze at myself for hours and hours:
	My mirror, you see, has magic powers:
	When I speak to my mirror it speaks to
	me…
SNOW WHITE	She's soft in the head, as you can see.
QUEEN	You nasty child! Don't be so rude!
	You're jealous of my pulchritude!

SNOW WHITE	Now that's an ambiguous sort of word.
	Coming from you it's quite absurd!
	We know you think that you are pretty…
	Such self-deception is a pity.
	Osama bin Laden's just like you…
	You'd make a lovely couple too!…
QUEEN	Now, that's enough! Once and for all
	Mirror, mirror on the wall
	(Actually its in my hand!)
	Who is the fairest in the land?
COM PERE	Snow white, you nit wit! Eee, she's grand!
SNOW WHITE	Snow White? Whoever can that be?
	I do believe… why, yes! That's me!
QUEEN	My magic mirror's never wrong -
	I am undone! But not for long!
	I'll rid me of this adversary
	And then some handsome man I'll marry.
	With Snow White dead there'll be no risk -
	oh!
	I'll be the belle of the local disco!
	While she will be in an early grave.
	Where is my huntsman, tall and brave?
	Take this girl upon your charger
	And in the woods you may dispatch her!
COMPERE	And so the huntsman took Snow White.
	She wouldn't give in without a fight.
	So he went off and shot a deer
	And left Snow White all lonesome there.
	Through thorn and copse she stumbled
	round
	But then a little cottage found.

SNOW WHITE	That's a bit of luck, I ween,. I shall be safe here from the Queen. The owner will be glad to see A pretty au-pair girl like me.
COMPERE	She stepped inside and looked with horror At all the awful mess, begorrah, Broken bottles, empty kegs, Fag ends stubbed out in fried eggs, Dirty plates piled in the sink, And over all, a nasty stink.
SNOW WHITE	Phew! This place is somewhat niffy! I'll get it ship-shape in a jiffy. There - that's all done! Now off I'll go And have a little rest. Hey-ho!
COMPERE	Up the winding stair she rambles And finds the bedroom in a shambles. Seven beds she makes, and then Goes to sleep… at half-past ten? At five o'clock we hear the sound Of fourteen footsteps on the ground. Can it be the seven dwarves? Wearing little hats and scarves… (you find a rhyme for dwarves, then!) Amazed to find the house so clean They wonder if a fairy's been? One dwarf cries out, with face all red "There's a little girlie in my bed!"
SNOW WHITE	Hallo, small person, don't be fright: I'll introduce myself - Snow White. The wicked Queen has turned me out! May I stay here?…
COMPERE	… "Yes please!" they shout.

SNOW WHITE	How very kind! I'll be your friend And all your little socks will mend. I'll cook your dinners, clean your shoes, Wash your shirts and iron your trews, Keep the cottage shining bright, And give you Horlicks every night!
COMPERE	And so Snow White began her stay…
QUEEN	It's time I had some lines to say! (We noticed from the very start You gave yourself the biggest part!) Meanwhile dear friends, you may recall, That blasted mirror on the wall? It tells me that Snow White stays put with seven little men… tut tut!! My moral soul is filled with shame That she should taint the family name When I have tried in vain for years! Revenge is sweet - I'll shed no tears But in disguise I now go thither And poisoned apples I will give her! (What a dreadful rhyme!)
COMPERE	…… …. there's plenty more!
QUEEN	So now I'm knocking at the door.
SNOW WHITE	Who's there? Good gracious, bless my soul, It's Myra Hindley on parole! Pray do come in and wipe your feet. Do you bring something nice to eat?

QUEEN

She must not see through my disguise,
I think a change of voice is wise.
Lovely lady, pray come near,
I'm just a poor old gypsy, dear.
Just cross my palm with fifty p
And I'll read what fortune comes to thee.
Aha, I see a wondrous thing!
United win the Cup next spring!
The pound will fall and rise again
With David Cameron at No Ten.
Now into my basket just dip in
And try a Cox's Orange Pippin…
Are they not tasty, round and red?
Now in a minute you'll be dead!

COMPERE

Snow White took a bite and hit the floor -
The Queen went cackling out the door.
That night the little dwarves came home -
You should have heard them wail and moan!
"Snow White - she's dead! How cold she feels…
Can we apply for meals-on-wheels?
We'll build for her a crystal tomb
  Up on the hill where there's more room."
  And so they laid the lovely lass
  Like a cucumber, under glass…
  They knelt around, and said a prayer.
  But lo! Who is that handsome man
Whose anxious eyes this scene doth scan!
  The Prince! He looks into the casket
And wonders bravely dare he ask it?
Just one kiss upon her forehead?
One kiss… and she does something horrid.
She spits the apple out again
Then sits up smiling, right as rain.

SNOW WHITE   Oh handsome Prince - you've saved my life!
      Now you must take me for your wife.
      And let these dwarves of whom I'm fond
      Sit round the Palace goldfish pond

COMPERE   So they were wed! Oh frabjous joy!
      They had twelve children, one a boy,
      And every Christmas Snow White sends
      Seven hoodies to her little friends.
      Our play is done - but ere we flit
      The Queen's got her dramatic bit.

QUEEN   (Thank you, dear.)
      Blow winds, and crack your cheeks!
      Fire burn and bubble and squeaks!
      Lightning splinter through the sky -
      Snow White lives, so I must die!
      See this knife? Now I will force it
      Deep into my whalebone corset...
      Ugh... tis done!... I'll say farewell!...
      So give us a clap... didn't we do well?

CHURCH BELLES
– by Carol Reeve –

Adapted for radio

Church bells are reminding the village faithful to leave the warmth of their firesides and gather together in the unheated church. So the play opens to the sound of Church bells pealing. Footsteps crunching slowly on gravel, and heavy breathing.

MABEL	Nearly there, dear. We're in good time anyway.
NELLIE	Thank goodness. I'm sure this hill gets steeper every week.
MABEL	I know it does, dear! Wipe your feet. We're not the first, anyway.

Sound of footsteps on stone floor

NELLIE	The Watsons are here already – at least they're not sitting in our pew!
MABEL	They must have taken the hint. You were a bit aggressive, dear, last week.
	In you go - shove up.
NELLIE	Put your bag next to mine, so no one else will come and sit in here
MABEL	Just let me get my humbugs out first. Don't want to cough during the sermon. Wonder what his theme will be this week – obesity, I shouldn't doubt. Plenty of examples of it in here today.

Short silence while they look around

MABEL	She's got a different hat on today.
NELLIE	Who has?
MABEL	Her over there. Last week it was a sort of hand-knitted beret, all different colours.
NELLIE	Sounds awful.
MABEL	It was – don't you remember? This one is much smarter. Some sort of fur.
NELLIE	Rabbit I expect. Her husband keeps rabbits.
MABEL	Does he? How do you know?
NELLIE	They live near me, and he keeps them in a hutch in the garden. Every now and again they escape and eat up my lettuces.
MABEL	So you know her then, her with the fur hat?
NELLIE	Never spoken to her. My neighbour on the other side hasn't got a good word to say for her.
MABEL	Well, well, She does look a bit sour, I must say.
NELLIE	Hush – she's turned round… Good morning, Mrs. Brown! Nice hat, dear!
MABEL	Ooh Nellie, you are awful!
NELLIE	That's her husband sitting beside her – he's got his feet on that nice new kneeler!
MABEL	Ooh, that's naughty. I hope his shoes are clean.
NELLIE	I don't think he's been to church before. She's usually on her own.

MABEL	Perhaps he's feeling guilty about something – like killing his innocent little rabbits to make her a new hat!
NELLIE	Oh look! Mrs Roberts has just come in – give her a big smile – poor thing. She is being very brave.
MABEL	Yes – forty years married and he goes off with that kennel maid - no sense of decency.
NELLIE	No, you're right. Somebody told me that she cut up all his suits and threw them in the dustbin!
MABEL	Good for her! I would have done the same in her situation. Mine was a bit different, of course. Fred went off with his push bike and he never came back. I just said Good Riddance!
NELLIE	Do you ever hear from him?
MABEL	No – never, not a word. Mind you I'm still getting his pension every week!
NELLIE	And so you should. Vicar should be here soon – I do enjoy our Sunday morning gossip, Mabel!
MABEL	So do I! Mind you, they're all probably gossiping about us! Do you think they know about our trip to see those gorgeous Chippendales?
NELLIE	Hush dear! Stand up – the Vicar's just coming. Doesn't he look wholesome in his new surplice?

Sound of several people standing up as church organ begins to play "Let us with a gladsome mind… "
The Hymn fades away and there is a short pause. Then a final hymn comes to an end, and we hear the chatter of people leaving, saying goodbye to the vicar at the door.

MABEL   What a lovely service, wasn't it, Nellie? Such a pity poor old Mr Wilkins had such a bad turn during prayers, all over the floor. Something his daughter gave him for breakfast, no doubt. I don't think many people noticed though.

NELLIE   But what about that sermon, Mabel? I didn't know where to look when he began talking about adultery, but I noticed that Mrs Roberts was smiling all the way through.

MABEL   Mr and Mrs Brown are leaving – look! His face is almost purple, and she is practically pushing him out of the door! If we're quick we shall catch them up!

NELLIE   There they are – and talking to Mrs Roberts… Oh, did you see that? Mrs Brown gave Mrs Roberts a might whack in the face! And Mr Brown is taking Mrs Roberts' arm and leading her away… You must have been right, Mabel – he did feel guilty and now we know why!

MABEL   Watch out – Mrs Brown has taken off her fur hat… and thrown it at the Vicar! She obviously didn't approve of his sermon either.

NELLIE   Well, it was a bit insensitive, considering
                the situation. Perhaps the Vicar didn't
                know about all the goings on!

MABEL   Well, he does now! Goodbye, Vicar, thank
                you so much for such a lovely sermon.
                No, I don't think Mrs. Brown wants her
                hat back – if you like, I'll take it off you
                and put it in the Jumble Sale on Saturday.
                Oh – thank you.

NELLIE   Goodbye, Vicar, see you next Sunday.
                Come on, Mabel, we'll pop into the
                Crown on the way back and tell everyone
                in there what they've missed!

*Sound of footsteps hurrying on gravel – suitable music and fade
out.*

Carol Reeve

THE LETTER
– by Carol Reeve –

CHARACTERS
Ruth
Mama
Fred

Scene opens: Mama is slumped in a chair centre stage, a letter in her hand. Enter daughter Ruth, singing, with a bunch of flowers. Sees Mama and kneels beside her.

RUTH   O my Mama! You look so sad!
Are you unwell? Are your rheumatics bad?

MAMA   My dearest child – alas, my end is near,
My days are surely numbered now, I fear.
Your dear Papa awaits beyond the grave,
And you must try to be extremely brave.
But do not weep, for I have wondrous news:
This letter, dear, will chase away your blues.

RUTH   Papa would be so pleased to see you smile!
I'll read your letter in a little while.
But first, Mama, I can no longer hide
That I have something secret to confide.

MAMA   Not now, my dear, your news will have to wait,
The portent of these lines is far too great,
As you, my child will shortly understand.
Lord Criccieth has asked me for your hand!

(Ruth gasps in horror)

MAMA   This means that all his wealth and huge estate
He'll hand to you, my dearest, on a plate!
Now I can die in peace and know for sure
That you will want for nothing ever more.

RUTH   Alas, alas, Mama, it cannot be!
I know him not, and he knows nought of me.
Besides, my heart is given to another
And I would sooner die than lose my lover.

MAMA   What talk is this? Who dares to woo my daughter?

RUTH   His name is Fred, and he's a railway porter.

MAMA   It can't be true! You shameless, wicked girl,
How could you think of marrying a churl?
You're throwing all away, it seems to me!
… and what shall I say in answer to Lord C?

(Enter Fred)

RUTH   *(to Fred)* My darling Fred! Alas, we cannot marry
Without my mother's blessing and a dowry.
It seems another suitor's made a claim:
My mother would prefer I take HIS name.

FRED

Fear not, my love, we never shall be parted,
I cannot bear to see you so downhearted.
Forgive me, Ma'am, and you too, dearest Ruth,
For being economical with the truth:
To gain the true affection of your daughter
I took the lowly job of railway porter.
But now I know for sure that she loves me
I can reveal … Lord Criccieth! I am he!

(gasps, embracings and congratulations all round. Mama rises and faces audience)

MAMA

This little story has a happy ending –
I find my aches and pains are quickly mending,
I'll live to see my daughter wed this rascal…
Then I'll move in with them into the Castle!

(all bow)

Carol Reeve

THE BRONTE SISTERS
– by Carol Reeve –

The parlour of the Parsonage at Haworth. Charlotte is dusting the bookshelves and the sideboard, and accidentally knocks a little notebook onto the floor. She picks it up, and begins to read. She is so intrigued that at first she is not aware that Ann has entered the room. She turns hurriedly, holding the notebook behind her back, but sighs with relief when she sees her sister.

CHARLOTTE Oh, Ann! You surprised me – I was not at first aware that anyone had entered the room. But look – I found this notebook quite by chance. It contains several poems, all in Emily's hand. They are so vigorous, so terse – not at all like poetry usually written by a woman. They have a peculiar music, a wild melancholy and so elevating. They should be published!

(Emily has entered the room, as Charlotte is still speaking, and sees the notebook in her hand.)

EMILY What are you doing, Charlotte? That book is mine – you are very impertinent to pry into my private matters. Give it back to me at once!

ANN I'm sure Charlotte meant no harm. Emily.

CHARLOTTE   Indeed I did not. Please forgive me, but my eye was drawn to these moving stanzas. "No coward soul is mine, no trembler in the world's storm-troubled sphere!" They deserve to be seen by the world, Emily! Let me send them to be published?

(Emily snatches the notebook away)

EMILY   Never!

CHARLOTTE   Perhaps with a few of my own poor verses, which as you already know I have long struggled to compose.

ANN   That would be a splendid plan, Charlotte! Now I have a confession to make to you both – I too have felt constrained to write some sad lines upon the death of Papa's dear curate, Mr. Weightman.

CHARLOTTE   Oh my poor love! You cared for him so dearly, yet he was never aware of your true feelings for him. Please read your verses to us, Ann.

(Ann looks sadly toward Emily, who slowly nods her head. Ann goes to a drawer and takes out a small booklet)

ANN   Very well. I have called my poem
"Reminiscence".

    Yes, thou art gone! And never more
    Thy sunny smile shall gladden me:
    But I may pass the old church door
    And pace the floor that covers thee.
    May stand upon the cold, damp stone
    And think that, frozen, lies below
    The lightest heart that I have known,
    The kindest I shall ever know.

Yet, though I cannot see thee more,
'Tis still a comfort to have seen:
And though thy transient life is o'er
'Tis sweet to think that thou hast been.
To think a soul so near divine
Within a form so angel fair,
United to a heart like thine,
Has gladdened once our humble sphere.

(The sisters are greatly moved, and hug each other. Then Charlotte goes and retrieves her little notebook.)

CHARLOTTE.   Let me read to you my poem that I have
entitled LIFE. Perhaps it will gladden your
heart a little, Ann.
Life, believe, is not a dream
So dark as sages say:
Oft a little morning rain
Foretells a pleasant day.
Sometimes there are clouds of gloom,
But these are transient all;
If the shower will make the roses bloom
O why lament its fall?
Rapidly, merrily,
Life's sunny hours flit by,
Gratefully, cheerily,
Enjoy them as they fly!
What though death at times steps in
And calls our best away?
What though sorrow seems to win
O'er hope, a heavy sway?
Yet hope again elastic springs
Unconquered, though she fell,
Still buoyant are her golden wings,
Still strong to bear us well.
Manfully, fearlessly,
The day of trial bear,

> For gloriously, victoriously,
> Can courage quell despair!

(Now the sisters are relaxed and smiling, so Emily stands a little apart from them, and opens her notebook. She too begins to read)

EMILY   This poem is also about love, and it is perhaps full of rare passion, which I cannot excuse, except to say that when I stand on the wind-swept hills, I am so moved by God's love that I have to pour out these feelings into my little notebook.
No coward soul is mine,
No trembler in the world's storm-troubled sphere!
I see Heaven's glories shine,
And Faith shines equal, arming me from fear.
O God within my breast,
Almighty, ever-present Deity!
Life, that in me has rest,
As I, undying Life, have power in Thee!
Vain are the thousand creeds
That move men's hearts, unutterably vain,
Worthless as withered weeds,
Or idlest froth amid the boundless main,
To waken doubt in one
Holding so fast by thy infinity,
So surely anchored on
The steadfast rock of Immortality.
With wide-embracing love
Thy spirit animates eternal years,
Pervades and broods above,
Changes, sustains, dissolves, creates and rears.
Though earth and moon were gone,
And suns and universes ceased to be,

And thou were left alone,
Every existence would exist in Thee.
There is not room for Death
Nor atom that his might could render
void,
Since Thou art Being and Breath
And what Thou art may never be
destroyed.

(The girls stand silently for a moment, then come close together)

CHARLOTTE Am I not right, sisters? Between us we have written some beautiful lines. We should publish our verses.

EMILY But no-one would contemplate publishing women's writings, my dear.

ANN Perhaps if we conceal our true names – find new identities which would protect us all from the shame of publicity

CHARLOTTE Or the fame perhaps? Our brother Bramwell used the name Northangerland when he published his verses four years ago. We must choose names for ourselves.

EMILY We could borrow Mr Arthur Nicholls middle name, as it begins with B – What think you of the sisters Bell?

ANN And keep our own initials! Ann – Anthony – no, Acton. Yes, I shall be Acton Bell.

CHARLOTTE Indeed Acton Bell does have a mysterious ring to it! I shall choose… Charles? Or Christopher? No – Currer – that's it! Currer which signifies nothing at all!

EMILY   Then if I MUST take part in this charade,
                 I wish to be known as Ellis Bell – very
                 nearly a gentleman, don't you agree? *(They
                 laugh, join hands in a circle calling happily*
                 Good evening, Mr Acton – Good Day, Mr
                 Ellis! --Your servant, Master Currer!

THE VERSION OF MAVIS
or
THE TIPSY ACTRESS AND THE PROMPTER

The erstwhile star of the amateur stage is preparing for her role as Portia in The Merchant of Venice. A large but empty bottle of sherry sits on her dressing table. The prompter pops her head round the door.

PROMPT   I see you're preparing for tonight's performance in good time, Mavis!

MAVIS   Shjust got to finish off this last drop of sherry – steadies the nerves, you know. But while I'm getting ready, would you just go through my big speech with me again ? I don't want to make a hash of it in front of Helen Mirren.

PROMPT   Helen Mirren? Is she out there, in the audience?

MAVIS   I've no idea, but anything's possible.

PROMPT   Okay. Are you ready?

MAVIS   Of course. The quantity of…

PROMPT   The quality of mercy is not strained.

MAVIS   Ah yes!

PROMPT   It droppeth like the gentle rain from heaven upon the place beneath.

MAVIS   He hoppeth like a gentleman from Devon upon the bracing heath.

PROMPT	It is twice blessed.
MAVIS	He is quite stressed.
PROMPT	It blesseth him that gives and him that takes.
MAVIS	He stresses primitives and (hic!) fairy cakes.
PROMPT	(*becoming more and more alarmed*) Tis mightiest in the mightiest.
MAVIS	He's flightiest in his nightiest…
PROMPT	It becomes the throned monarch…
MAVIS	He becomes a stoned tonic…
PROMPT	Better than his crown.
MAVIS	Better than a clown… (*she smiles broadly, bows to an imaginary audience and collapses onto a chair, where she falls asleep*)
PROMPT	Mavis! Mavis! Oh, dear, she's passed out. And we don't have an understudy! I shall have to play Portia myself! Mr Producer! Mr Producer! Help! (*and she runs off stage.*)

MONOLOGUES

MOTHER'S DAY

– by Carol Reeve –

*(The old lady is sitting in her room at the Nursing Home,
all alone, and feeling aggrieved.
It is Mother's Day and she has not heard from her family)*

Well, some happy Mothers Day this has turned out to be! There I was, chatting to that old Mr. Stanley over a cup of tea. and Matron comes across and bans me from the Residents Lounge for bad behaviour. Well, today of all days. All I did was ask him if he'd like a tart or a bit of crumpet? Funny, though - he went all puce and nearly swallowed his dentures. Goodness knows what he thought I'd meant. And then I said to old Mrs. Watson that I thought her grandson looked a bit queer with that ear ring in his lughole, and when was he coming out... well, leaving college of course, what else? ... and Matron zooms up all hoity-toity and ticks me off for being rude and banishes me upstairs! What was rude about that? Now I KNOW what rude is - like that bus driver when I went to have my feet done at the clinic, before I came in here, and I asked him if he went all the way - well, you wouldn't believe what he said to me! Now that WAS rude!

So here I am, stuck in my room in this residential care home for the elderly -and they are all really old, believe me - two of them are centurions. And its Mothers Day. How many cards do you think I got? - not one. No cards, no presents, - nothing. Not even a telegram. Of course the family live miles away, but they could have made an effort just the same. My daughter wrote and said I ought to get a mobile - well, honestly, I may be in my second childhood but the last thing I want is a silly paper toy hanging over my bed! My grand kids didn't send me any drawings this year either - even they don't care. I shall just have to sit here, all gloomy, like Eeyore, waiting for Pooh and Piglet to bring me an empty honey pot and a burst balloon.

(Her attention is drawn to a noise outside,
and she goes to look out of the window)

There's a great big car just pulled up. Someone's got a visitor anyway. It's the same model as my daughter's car - in fact - why yes! It's her car! And she's brought the children to see me ... to see ME! Well, well, this is going to be a happy Mothers Day after all.

BY THE SEA
– by Carol Reeve –

Sandra is seated on a bench overlooking the sea.
She is holding a newspaper cutting in her hand.
She smiles gently at it. Then she looks towards the sea - then
shivers a little and turns quickly to her left. Her gaze fixes on
"someone" standing at the other end of the bench.

Anna ... Is that you, Anna? I was just thinking about you.
She smiles, and her gaze moves down as though watching "someone" coming to sit beside her.

This is where we first met, do you remember? Frinton on Sea, Easter 1983. John and I had booked into that B and B "Mon Repos" and you came with your mother during our last week. That Mrs. Perkins - ever so friendly and kind, but her cooking was atrocious! Your face when you first tasted her mutton stew! So we got talking, and then we three went for a walk together, and sat on this bench until we had to go in for tea. Then of course I had that accident the next day, when I slipped on the pebbly beach and twisted my ankle really bad. I couldn't put my weight on it, so I said I'd sit and chat with your mother while you and John went off and made the most of the lovely weather. I believe you two went for a swim and then sunbathed on the beach. When you got back, you both looked so happy, laughing and teasing - I thought John would never take his eyes off you.

The rest of the week was warm and sunny - but I couldn't go anywhere. At least you and John had a good time - but I remember seeing you two saying goodbye to each other just before our taxi came to take us to the station... you were crying... John didn't say much on the way home. He was very quiet for ... a long time.

And then two years later he was killed in that terrible car crash. You wrote me such a nice letter, and we kept in touch ever since. You never married, did you? And only last week I saw this notice in the paper... cancer was it? I wished I could have said goodbye, that I had known all along what happened between you and John. I loved him too, you see, so I did understand.

I booked to come back here after I read about... about you in the paper, just to come and remember for the last time.

She glances behind the ghost.

There's someone over there, Anna - - look! He's smiling - and waving to us... it looks like... yes, it is ! It's John. He's come to fetch you, Anna - you can be together at last. Go now, dear - and God bless.

"Anna" gets up - Sandra follows Anna with her eyes and lifts her hand in farewell. She watches "them" out of sight, then she turns back, lets the cutting slip onto the floor, gives a deep sigh and sits quite still while the curtain closes.

S.P.L.O.J.S.

– by Carol Reeve –

It gives me great pleasure to be here tonight, to tell you about the wonderful work being done by the Society for the Protection of Ladies Organising Jumble Sales – or, as everyone knows us, SPLOJ. At the end of a hectic day running a jumble sale, do you feel tired, irritable and depressed? What you need is SPLOJ. Running a jumble sale is like… feeding rhubarb to a sick elephant: all that effort hardly seems compensated by the solvency gained at the end.

SPLOJ's aim is to alluviate your problems by pooling our resources and finding a convenient solution. Some members of your committee may make alternative suggestions, such as sponsored curate affrighting… I beg your pardon, that should read sponsored karate fighting – or possibly doing Macbeth in the church hall. But you can jump the first hurdle by turning a deaf ear, pulling up your socks and hanging onto your principles. There will be no more haggling over Mrs. Poggles' hand-me-downs, no more rummaging dealers, no more gypsies, tramps, stray dogs or cockroaches. If you follow the SPLOJ code there will be no need for trestle tables, bouncers, or even Mrs. Blogg's colourful but rather ribald posters.

All you need is a few hundred carrier bags and a dozen stalwart maidens. It's really quite simple – you collect all the jumble together and spend a care-free half hour sorting it all into bundles – one shirt, one pair of trousers, one dress, one skirt, one pair of shoes, one pair of socks, one pair of frilly undies, and so on. Then on the top you put one paperback book, one battered lamp shade, one jelly mould, one toasting fork, or what-have-you… Each bundle is put into the carrier bag and lined up on the floor of the church hall. Then on the stroke of two, the public are allowed to enter one at a time, handed a full carrier bag in exchange for a five pound note, then shepherded straight out again. Isn't that splendid? So within ten minutes you have disposed of all your jumble and are richer by several hundred pounds! Best of all, there are no nasty flotsam and jetsam snagging the legs of trestle tables.

This is particularly important. I once attended a jumble sale organised in the old fashioned way, which had tragic consequences. A certain Miss Clara Plum, a frail little thing of advanced age, was prone to rummaging through the articles that had slipped to the ground. She was last seen trying on a pair of purple long johns whilst clutching a sequined camisole, with a bird cage on her head. When the last customer had departed, the committee allowed Jake Higgins, the rag and bone person, to remove all the unsold rubbish. Three weeks later at their next committee meeting, Mrs Fred Plum stood up and asked if anyone had seen her Auntie Clara who had vanished since the jumble sale. Then the Social Secretary read out a letter she had recently received from Mr. Higgins, enclosing a postal order for £2.50p. It read as follows:

"Dear Sir or Madam, Oi am returning the £2.50 what you guv me for all that gear wiv many fanks. The extra pension is coming in very handy. Yours, Jake Higgins esquire."

Thus the whereabouts of Miss Plum was ascertained to everyone's relief.

Jumble sales are full of pitfalls –you clamber out of one only to tumble into the next. So long as you ladies will insist on displaying your goods on trestle tables, your charitable aims will be prostrated and you will be undone.

But SPLOJ is here to uplift your outlook. Our leaflet gives sound advice based on the experiences of our members, many of whom had come to grief through faulty planning. I leave you with the sincere hope that your next Jumble Sale will be a tremendous success, indeed a solid semblance of SPLOJ...

THE THESPIAN HISTRIONICUS

– by Carol Reeve –

My talk tonight concerns that most interesting member of the bird family, the Thespian Histrionicus, known to us all as the Actor. Instantly recognisable by its habit of strutting and fretting, the plumage of the male actor varies between gaudy waist coats and faded jeans, depending on its location, and its aptitude for catching the early worm.

Its song is particularly interesting, as it is easily heard above the general hub-hub of a tube train, for example, because of its exquisite modulation and carefully rounded vowel sounds.

The Northern Actor however has a tendency to elongate certain tones, while roosting in its natural environment, but quickly changes its tune during southern migration. This is true of all Thespians who originate north of a line from the Watford Palace to the Bristol Hippodrome, but overseas migrants such as the Australian Bushwacker, retain their individuality come what may, with the rather raucous call "Good on yer, mate".

As for the diminutive Cockney Thespian, he can be heard any time your Lambeth way if it wasn't for the 'ouses in between.

Most actors are born (generally between scenes in a dressing room) and quickly learn to follow their parents onto the boards. Most fledglings learn to strut and fret at a very young age and, once they have assumed their true feathers, they are launched into the outside world (or rat race as it is sometimes known) to spend many happy hours queuing at auditions, soup kitchens and Job Centres.

At this stage in their lives, many females of the species, known as Actresses, become secretary birds, or just broody; they hibernate and are not seen for many years until they suddenly reappear with a dear little fledgling groomed to become one of fifty seven varieties.

Nowadays, the Actors have been able to further their careers by appearing "on the box", and even the less successful ones can become Extra-verts, or walk-ons. But those at the top of the tree, however, should beware - it is quicker falling down than it was getting up, and the toughest of birds may find it has to spend many months quietly resting.

The character of the Thespian Histrionicus is much like that of the starling: it is a gregarious creature, but tends to peck and shove quite viciously when the pickings are few.

The most common variety of Actor is the Amateur Dramaticus Histrionicus - large flocks are to be found roosting in village halls, community centres, hay barns etc., where their ritual displays at irregular intervals draw crowds of twitchers from far and wide.

Unfortunately the Actor is often regarded as an oddity by members of the general public, due probably to its habit of posing whenever it sees a CCTV or speed camera, and of calling all other birds "darling!" But how dull life would be without these colourful creatures!